Everyday Life of the Incas

Opposite: View of Machu Picchu

ANN KENDALL

Everyday Life of

THE INCAS

DRAWINGS AND PHOTOGRAPHS
BY THE AUTHOR

DORSET PRESS
New York

This edition published by Dorset Press,
a division of Marboro Books Corporation,
by arrangement with B.T. Batsford Ltd.
1989 Dorset Press

ISBN 0-88029-350-0
(formerly ISBN 0-7134-1072-8)

Printed in the United States of America
M   9 8 7 6 5 4 3 2 1

To my parents
Elizabeth and Kenneth Kendall
who lived for many years
in South America

ACKNOWLEDGEMENT

The author wishes to thank the Winston Churchill Memorial Trust for a fellowship to Peru in 1968, which laid the foundations for specialization in this field of study; the generous assistance of Mr Colin Cannon in the preparation of the text and illustrations; Dr M. Chávez Ballón, Professor of Archaeology at the University of Cuzco, and Dr R. T. Zuidema, Professor of Anthropology at the University of Illinois, Urbana, conversations with whom have been instructive and stimulating in the past; kind friends in Peru, especially the Zavaleta family of Cuzco; also, Dr W. Bray for reading the manuscript and Mr Peter Kemmis Betty, representing the Publishers.

The Author and Publishers wish to thank the Musée de L'Homme, for permission to reproduce the jacket illustration; Dr R. T. Zuidema for illustrations (86), (91); The Institut d'Ethnologie, Paris, acknowledging the debt owed to Guaman Poma's illustrated chronicle; Emilio Harth-Terré on whose plans (45), (52) are based; Dr M. Chávez Ballón and the Patronato de Arqueología del Cuzco, on whose work (43) is based; The Museo Arqueologico, Cuzco, and the Museo Nacional de Antropología, Lima, for permission to photograph specimens (13), (14), (34), (38), (48) and (17), (19), (20), (37), (47), (74), (75), respectively.

Also the Publishers wish to thank the following publishers for permission to quote from: University of Oklahoma Press *The Incas of Pedro Cieza de Leon*, by Pedro Cieza de Leon, translated by Harriet de Onis, 1959; University of Texas Press, *Royal Commentaries of the Incas*, by Garcilaso de la Vega, translated by H. W. Livermore 1966; Penguin Books Ltd, *The Discovery and Conquest of Peru* by Augustin de Zarate translated by J. M. Cohen. Copyright © J. M. Cohen, 1968. Dr J. H. Rowe 'Inca Culture at the time of the Spanish conquest', 1946. Where quotations appear they are acknowledged to their author.

The Inca social hierarchy

CONTENTS

7

THE ILLUSTRATIONS

GLOSSARY

Aclla	Virgin, Chosen Woman
Acllahuasi	House of the Virgins, and Chosen Women
Alpaca	Cameloid
Amauta	Elder or wise-man
Antisuyu	Quarter of Cuzco and of the Inca empire (Eastern Forest Tribes)
Aymara	People, language
Ayllu	Community group (social, kin or local group)
Cayao	Generic name of ayllu
Charqui	Jerked meat
Chasqui	Runner, post
Chicha	Fermented drink, usually made from maize beer
Chinchaysuyu	Quarter of Cuzco and of the Inca empire
Chullpa	House of the Dead
Chuño	Dehydrated potato
Citua	Religious festival
Coca	Low tropical bush whose leaves are used as a stimulant
Collana	Generic name of ayllu
Coya	Title, Queen or Empress
Cumbi	Finest tapestry cloth
Cuntisuyu	Quarter of Cuzco and of the Inca empire
Curaca	Native leader or lord
Cuzco	Inca capital
Guanaco	Wild cameloid
Guanqui	'Brother', guardian spirit
Hanan, Hurin	Moieties of bi-partite division
Huaca	Shrine, holy
Huanacauri	Mountain shrine

Kero	Drinking cup
Llama	Cameloid
Mamacuna	Consecrated Virgin or Chosen Woman
Mit'a	Public works service
Mitayo	Servant
Mitima(es)	Colonist(s)
Montaña	Forested hills of the Eastern Andes
Panaca	Royal lineage
Payan	Generic name of ayllu
Puma	Mountain lion, jaguar
Puna	High treeless plateau
Quechua	People, language
Quinua	Highland grain
Quipu	Knotted cords
Quipucamayoc	Keeper of knotted cords, accountant
Selva	Jungle
Tambo	Inn, shelter on highway
Tocricoc Apu	Inca provincial governor
Usnu	Platform structure, throne
Vicuña	Wild cameloid
Visacha	Large rodent
Yanacona	Class of government servants
Yachahuasi	House of Teaching

PREFACE

The Inca empire, which extended over the Andean area of South America some 3,500 kilometres (2,200 miles) from the north west to the south east and about 320 kilometres (200 miles) in width, was discovered by the Spanish after they had already conquered Mexico and most of Central America. Francisco Pizarro, a Spanish adventurer, organized the first landing in what is now Peru.

In 1532 Pizarro, with a small force of men and horses, reached Cajamarca, where the Inca ruler Atahuallpa was encamped with his army. With considerable cunning and using a brutal strategy Pizarro succeeded in kidnapping Atahuallpa, making him a hostage, and thus acquired power over the Inca empire.

After 1539, when the conquest was finally secured and the initial excitement over the procuring of quantities of gold and other riches was waning, one of the first problems facing the Spaniards was how to rule over the vast area which had been under Inca rule and which had an estimated population of about seven million. It was necessary to find out as much as possible about the Inca organization of the area, its resources and the tax contributions made to the Incas.

The Incas had no written histories or accounts of their organization which could be used by the Spaniards. The latter therefore had to prepare their own accounts which were based on their observations and informants who were either descendants of the Incas or indians from the subject provinces. These accounts vary in reliability and the chroniclers have been criticized for their misrepresentation of information which they interpreted in the light of their own culture. Although there are difficulties in disentangling the historical accounts from traditions relating to theoretical organization, the picture of daily life under the Incas, described by past historians and recent scholars of many biases, remains available to us at its face value in the original accounts.

Original historical and descriptive accounts generally considered to be most useful and reliable include the earliest eye-witnesses: Miguel de Estete, Pedro Sancho de la Hoz, Francisco de Jerez. Agustín de Zárate, who though he wrote from the point of view of the second Peruvian generation, drew first-hand information from Pizarro's comrades. Some of the best-known

14

early sources later used by many historians are Pedro Cieza de León, Juan de Betanzos, Juan Polo de Ondegardo, Martin de Murúa, Fernando de Santillan, and Pedro Sarmiento de Gamboa. Written in the seventeenth century, Bernabé Cobo's work is considered one of the most reliable and has a reasonable and credible style. Three interesting, though not necessarily always very reliable, works are by Peruvian and *mestizo* chroniclers: Garcilaso de la Vega and Juan de Santacruz Pachacuti Yamqui Salcamaygua wrote early in the seventeenth century, and in 1661 Felipe Guaman Poma de Ayala wrote an attractive illustrated chronicle. The drawings in Poma's account contain much detailed information on all areas of Inca life and I have found them an invaluable source on which to base many of the illustrations in this book. There are also a number of valuable accounts primarily concerned with the religon of the Incas and that of their subjects; the earliest of these is that by Cristobal de Molina (El Cuzqueno). For research, some of the most valuable sources of data today are the local community archives and the local reports of the Spanish administrators and inspectors, which are still being found in national archives and libraries.

All this adds up to a wealth of descriptive and sometimes conflicting information, which is most authoritatively dealt with in *Inca Culture* by Dr John Howland Rowe, written in 1946. A more recent view of the historical interpretation contained in the original works and its subsequent effect on Inca organization has been put forward by Dr R. T. Zuidema in *The Ceque System of Cuzco*, published in 1964. Although Zuidema's approach conflicts with that of Rowe in its view of the significance of early Inca history, it does not however disagree basically with Rowe's view of later history, nor of Inca organization, but tends to clarify and illumine certain of the more complex aspects of it. In addition, the work of Dr J. V. Murra, among others, has contributed to a better understanding of certain aspects of Inca culture.

Archaeology, while an essential tool in reconstructing pre-Inca cultures and for checking the extent of Inca domination and influence in the Andean area, has not been effectively applied in enough areas for evaluating the historical and cultural data recorded. For instance, if we wish to know exactly how an indian lived in his abode, where he ate, and where his wife cooked his meals, we have to search the records for data and will succeed in obtaining only generalized references with no specific information.

In such cases, where clear evidence is not forthcoming from another source, I shall rely on my own field study and research on Inca architecture and planning. Also, occasionally, anthropological and ethnographic sources can be used to throw light on scanty descriptions in order to clarify practical points.

I have not followed any consistent pattern in the spelling of Andean names. In the Romanization of Inca names and words in the Inca language (Quechua) I have usually adopted the most frequently used Spanish spelling.* The use of the word Inca itself can become confusing. Inca is the name of the *Inca* tribe, whose leader was also called Inca. The plural use of the word covers more general usage—including the Inca nobility who were all Incas by birth, also others who were 'Incas by privilege'. (In addition, the word Inca can be used as an adjective.) I shall refer therefore to the *Inca* tribe and the ruler Inca in the singular before the expansion into an empire, and subsequently to the ruling class as the 'Incas' and the Inca himself either by name or by one of his titles, for instance Emperor, or Sapa Inca.

* Although there is considerable variation in Spanish spelling and interpretation of Quechua words, the following are some of the most usual differences between the indian words as written in Quechua and Spanish:
k — q(u) or g
q — c
w — hu or gu
o — u
y — i (at the beginning of a word)
e — i
s — x, c, or j
r — l
p — b

Everyday Life of the Incas

The land and its history

MAN'S ARRIVAL IN AMERICA.

There is no evidence to suggest that the American continent was inhabited by man prior to his *homo sapiens* stage of development and man's arrival in the Americas is thought to have occurred by approximately 25,000 BC.

The first arrivals were migrant hunters, of mongoloid race. They entered the continent from Asia, in pursuit of mammoth and other pleistocene game, by crossing the Bering Straits, which during the ice ages formed a land bridge with the Aleutian Islands between North-east Asia and North America. Eventually they found their way to Alaska and then south through Canada via the great glacial valleys. It is probable that ice at the foot of the Canadian Rockies blocked this passage during certain periods and it is believed that it was probably blocked between 23,000–10,000 BC, so that relatively few migrants passed through prior to this period and the main migration occurred after 10,000 BC.

After gaining access, small groups of people moved slowly south to hunt in many areas of the vast new continent. Until recently reliable archaeological evidence placed the presence of pleistocene hunters in California by 15,000 BC and at the tip of South America by 9000 BC. However Dr R. S. MacNeish, who leads the Ayacucho Archaeological-Botanical Project, has suggested on the basis of radiocarbon dates obtained, that man occupied the Andean area as early as 22,000 years ago. No doubt correspondingly earlier dates will soon be obtained for North America and Central America. The earliest migrants to the Andean area filtered from north to south through the highlands and coastal regions—where the jungle growth was not too dense—to populate extremely diverse environments and climates in the area which was later to be dominated by the *Inca*.

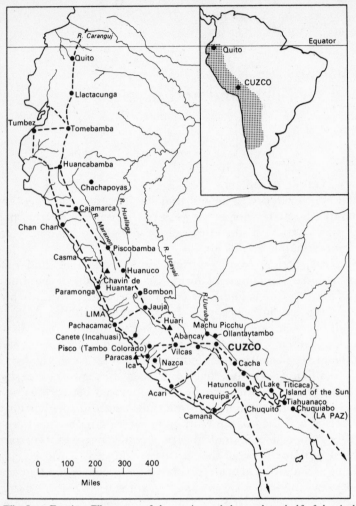

*1 The Inca Empire. The extent of the empire and the northern half of the Andean
area, showing the main roads and towns*

At the end of the pleistocene, by 9000 BC in North America and
slightly later in South America, the large animals became
extinct. With their decline possibilities for hunting ceased to be
satisfactory and man had to learn to supplement his diet from
other sources. By 5000 BC in some parts of Mexico and the Andean
areas (food gathering techniques were already anticipating
agricultural development), a more settled way of life was to

result and after 2500 BC there were considerable increases in local populations due to a steadier and expanding supply of food.

GEOGRAPHICAL DESCRIPTION OF THE ANDEAN AREA

The everyday life under Inca rule described in this book covers the period which saw the height of Inca achievement. The *Inca* concentrated all their effort on unification and in overcoming the difficulties of the environment with a Bronze Age technology. In order to do this they imposed a rigorous policy of organization which was carried out by a hierarchy of Inca administrators. The administrators and officials of any importance were Incas, that is, they belonged to the Inca class who had set themselves up as an élite, ruling nobility in an empire in which all subjects or commoners were the conquered peoples, except for the local chiefs, the *curacas*, who formed a subdivision of the élite class.

Developments in the Andean area leading up to the Inca period can be more easily understood after some consideration of its geographical characteristics. For our purpose the extent of the Andean area will be considered as that part of South America under Inca rule in the latter part of the fifteenth century and prior to the Spanish conquest in 1532. This area comprises Peru, Ecuador, Bolivia, North-west Argentina and the greater part of Chile, north of the River Maule. The capital of the Incas, Cuzco, is at the heart of the area, located in the Peruvian highlands (*1*).

This area, that the *Inca* were alone in being able to unify successfully, can be divided into three main geographical zones. Firstly, that of the warm, western desert strip bordering the Pacific Ocean. This coastal desert runs almost the full length of the area, except where the jungle intervenes in parts of Ecuador, becoming increasingly arid in Chile where it extends up into the highlands. The climate of this area is affected by the cold Humbolt current which flows along the coast causing mist, which hangs over the desert cooling it for many months of the year. The only indigenous plants in the desert are those of the *lomas* (areas of fog vegetation which lives off moisture in the air and once offered sustenance to early pre-agricultural settlers). The fauna of the coastal desert is meagre, consisting of lizards, foxes and field owls. Extensive oasis settlements have been able to survive here, where the many rivers descend from the Andes to flow into the sea. The coastal settlers eventually learnt to organize extensive irrigation schemes, using water sources from high in the river valleys to supply their fields, and also to use *puquios*—sunken

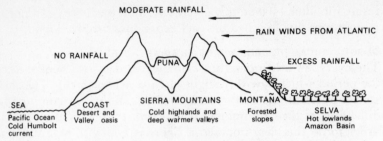

2 Diagram of west-east cross-section of the Andean area, showing the environmental and climatic conditions

fields dug near the water-table. Among the crops most success-fully grown on the coast were cotton, gourds, lima beans, squashes, chili-peppers, peanuts, guava, avocado and maize.

Throughout the Andean area, the climate varies more with elevation than with distance from the equator. Although mist gathers over the coast, there is normally no rainfall. The moisture in the air is retained and falls lightly in the highlands and heavily in the jungle zones (*2*).

The second geographical zone, that of the highlands, is formed by the parallel chains of the Andes descending from Colombia to Chile. The warmer temperate valleys and a few larger basins in the highlands supported small agricultural populations. Herds of alpaca, llama and vicuña were tended on the flat, cold, high *puna* tablelands between them. A large variety of crops have been adapted to grow at different altitudes since ancient times, so that maize, a chili-pepper and squash grew in the lower valley floors and slopes, alongside hardier root crops such as the potato and oca, and the grain quinoa—which can also be grown much higher. Certain varieties of potatoes can be grown as high as 4,000 metres (12,800 ft), but beyond this height only the tough low grasses and bushes can survive, providing grazing for cameloids which supplied the Andean peoples with wool and meat. There were often closer ties between the upper and lower ecological zones than between those on the same levels, since the mountains and tablelands form natural barriers between fertile valley pockets, which still impede the easy flow of com-munications (*3*).

A feature of the Andean highlands is that some of the rivers here have no outlet into the sea and form great salt pan lakes, sometimes covering large areas. The largest of these has dried up, resulting in the desert of Northern Chile (the Atacama desert), Western Bolivia and North-west Argentina. Another example— Lake Titicaca—has been an important centre in Andean pre-history. In the other areas of the highlands, there is much animal life including the *vicuña* and *guanuco* (wild cameloids), Andean deer, the puma and the *viscacha*, a large edible rodent.

The third zone, that of the jungle, can be divided up into two areas. First, the transitional area between the highlands and the jungle proper, which is called the *montaña*. This consists of higher forested slopes of the eastern Andes which are often shrouded in mist. The second area, the *selva*, is the swamp and insect-infested rain forest traversed by broad, slow-flowing rivers, which extends into the Amazon Basin. This forest caused as much horror among the *Inca* as it does to travellers today, so much so that one chronicler says the last outlawed Inca leader gave himself up to the Spaniards when they pursued him into the selva, 'rather than perish eating monkeys'. However, it is in the montaña valleys and the selva that many crops, particularly vegetables and fruits, could be most successfully grown. The Incas organized extensive cultivation and trade in these products, as well as in *coca* (leaves from which cochaine is extracted), manioc and tobacco grown in the montaña and the more accessible parts of the selva, east and north-east of Cuzco. The fauna of the montaña includes deer, bears, jaguars and as one descends to the selva, the whole varied fauna of the tropical rain forest: tapirs, monkeys, boas, peccaries and so on.

THE PRE-INCA CULTURES OF THE ANDEAN AREA

In the Andean area our knowledge of the pre-*Inca* occupations is based almost entirely on archaeological investigation. Recently the preliminary findings of the Ayacucho Archaeological-Botanical Project have culminated a decade's research by American, Peruvian, French, and Japanese archaeologists, to support the botanists' view 'that many of the plants first domesticated in western South America were indigenous to the highlands and that their domestication had probably first taken place in Peru'; also, that some plants were originally introduced into the highlands from the selva. At cave sites and open-air sites excavated in the Ayacucho valley, remains show evidence of successive cultures from 20,000 BC to AD 1500. Crude stone tools, including chopping tools reminiscent of types found in Asia were found in the lower levels of excavation in the Pikimachay (Flea) Cave. A quite different type of stone and bone tradition dating from about 9000 BC was found in the Jayamachay (Pepper) Cave, including projectile points (tips used for hunting). This 'Specialized Bifacial Point Tradition' is known to occur at other sites in the Andean area and elsewhere in the American continent.

Gradually during the period 8000–5000 BC there was an increase in seasonal gathering activities and the exploitation of the sea's resources on the coast. The domestication of plants in the highlands probably began after 5500 BC with the small-scale cultivation of quinoa, gourds and squash in the lower valleys. The llama and the guinea pig may already have been domesticated. Cotton, lucuma, primitive types of maize, sapindus fruits, tara and a type of bean start to appear after 4300 BC, and after 2800 BC more advanced types of maize and beans and probably root crops such as potatoes were being cultivated.

On the coast, while the sea's resources were being increasingly exploited, the lomas began to dry up—due to a change in the

3 Highland landscape, Calca valley near Cuzco

climate. This led to a movement of living sites to the shore and resulted in permanent settlements being created. Agriculture was introduced not only as a supplementary food source, but provided gourds and cotton, which were used as aids to fishing—for nets, floats and containers. Incipient agriculture occurs in three main stages on the Peruvian coast, which can be seen in increases in the number of crops cultivated culminating in the addition of maize c. 1500 BC, and in changes of house types. Ceramics began to replace gourd and basket containers in the north of Peru between 2000 and 1500 BC; these seem to have appeared first in Ecuador c. 3000 BC.

These developments in agriculture and the domestication of the llama and guinea pig took place in the final stages of the pre-ceramic period. The introduction of ceramics marks the beginning of the Initial period (1800–900 BC) and the first manifestations of social and religious organization in Peru. This is clearly seen in the architectural remains of the period.

Following the Initial period, in the Early Horizon (900–200 BC) some unification of ideas is reflected by the wide distribution of similar pottery motifs which provide us with evidence of the spread of religious concepts through the Chavin style. Chavin de Huántar, the type site in the Calleyon de Huayllas, was the most important of a number of ceremonial complexes of the Early Horizon. The main temple at this site shows several stages of rebuilding during the period and it was probably supported by a number of farming settlements in the region. Stone slabs functioning as cornices, lintels, corbels, tablets and obelisks, and objects of stone, bone and shell associated with the temple, were decorated with a great variety of elaborate cult images in that complex artistic tradition known as the Chavin style. Although this style was widespread in its influence, spreading from the north to the south coast and central highlands, there is, as yet, no evidence of this religious expansion having a corresponding militaristic expression, although its decline at the end of the period coincided with generally increased military activities in Peru.

After the Early Horizon there was a long period of regional development and technological experimentation (200 BC–AD 600), during which the Mochica (north coast) and the Nazca (south coast) cultures flourished and produced their famous pottery styles.

The large urban settlements of the Huari-Tiahuanaco

expansion were built in the Middle Horizon (AD 600–1000). Tiahuanaco, near Lake Titicaca in Bolivia, was the centre of an important religious cult whose main deity was depicted on the great monolithic doorway located there. Huari, in the southern Peruvian highlands, was evidently the capital of a militaristic empire which spread the Tiahuanaco religion over much of the territory of Peru later to be included in the more extensive Inca empire.

The Huari administration was evidently unable to rule successfully over the coastal and highland regions they had conquered. After the decline of the religious cult and the fall of the large urban centres at the end of the Middle Horizon, there followed another interim period, during which local styles and cultures came into their own again. There was a reversion to small isolated settlements in the southern highlands, and later, in the Inca period, small towns were built over much of the Andean area.

Only the Chimu built truly urban centres founded after the Middle Horizon, and the most important of these was the Chimu capital of Chanchan, situated on the northern Peruvian coast. This great centre was built shortly before the Inca period and covered some 28 square kilometres (12 square miles). The Chimu, who were a powerful state when the Incas began to build their empire, are considered to have had some impact on Inca culture.

THE BACKGROUND AND HISTORY OF THE INCA

During the Late Intermediate period (AD 1000–1483) the antecedents of the Incas were living in small tribes in the Cuzco region. The *Inca* were only one of many local groups. While there are gaps of knowledge in the chronology and development of the Cuzco region, some of the main phases of Peruvian archaeology can be recognized in the local pottery styles. Evidence of Huari influence exists in the southern end of the valley basin, at Pikillacta, approximately 30 kilometres (18 miles) south of Cuzco. There are, however, no traces of Huari architecture or ceramics in Cuzco itself, suggesting that it was not continuously inhabited in the Middle Horizon. The main pottery style, recognized in occupations of the period preceding that of the Inca Empire period, is generally called *Killke* and variations of this style are wide-spread between San Pedro de Cacha and Machu Picchu. The local development of the Inca is shown by the similarity of Killke to the standardized Inca style of the Empire period.

Partially preserved structures of the Late Intermediate period are found in hill sites where there is little attempt to adhere to any overall plan. Round and/or squarish structures are characteristic of this period and have little in common with Pikillacta. The Incas informed their Spanish conquerors that before they (the *Inca*) ruled, the peoples of the sierra were very diverse and disorganized and that they lived in inaccessible places because they were at constant war with each other.

The Early Inca period corresponds with a highly unreliable historical account in the records, estimated to be between AD 1200–1438. This covers the founding of the Inca dynasty up to 1438, when the *Inca* emerged as the most important state in the highlands.

Origin myths suggest the *Inca* consisted of three original lineage groups unified under the leadership of *Manco Capac*, the legendary founder of the dynasty. These myths describe the *Inca* searching for fertile land, which they found in the Cuzco valley, and their progress towards establishing themselves there.

On arriving in Cuzco the *Inca* were met with resistance and were forced to settle nearby until they succeeded in taking and occupying the site where they later built the famous Sun Temple, the Coricancha. Manco Capac is supposed to have reigned over the natives of the site of Cuzco only. After him the second and third Inca leaders, Sinchi Roca and Lloqui Yupanqui, are reported to have been peace-loving, while the fourth, Mayta Capac, caused bad feeling and a rebellion resulted amongst the inhabitants of Cuzco itself. The fifth, sixth and seventh Inca leaders made small conquests in the surrounding region (see list of Inca rulers, p. 211).

During this early period neither the *Inca* nor their neighbours organized their conquests, but instead periodically looted villages when there was danger of the people asserting themselves or when they seemed ripe for plunder. *Viracocha Inca*, the eighth ruler of the Inca dynasty, was the first to assume the title of *Sapa Inca* (Unique or Supreme Inca). He completed the local conquests, forming the *Inca* into a relatively small but powerful state. Events at the end of his reign were critical for the *Inca*, who were threatened from outside the Cuzco region on three sides.

In the south, the *Colla* and *Lupaca* tribes were great rivals, but fortunately, they kept each other busy while the *Inca* had to turn their attention west and north-west, to the *Quechua* and *Chanca* tribes. The *Inca* were on friendly terms with the Quechua, a powerful people whose territory acted as a convenient buffer between the *Inca* and the menacing Chanca. The latter were becoming increasingly powerful and had already conquered and settled in the province of Andahuayllas, formerly occupied by the Quechua. Faced with an inevitable future struggle with the powerful Chanca, Viracocha Inca strengthened the Inca situation by marrying the daughter of the chief of Anta, immediately northwest of Cuzco, and by making an alliance with the Quechua.

When the Chanca attack came, Viracocha was an old man and most of the *Inca* believed the Chanca were so strong that resistance would be useless. Viracocha and the heir, Inca Urcon, apparently fled Cuzco with their retinue. However, the day was saved by another group of Inca nobles and captains led by Yupanqui, also a son of Viracocha Inca, who called upon and got together as many allies as they could muster and successfully defended Cuzco from the Chanca attack. When the Chanca were subsequently defeated in a number of battles, the *Inca* found they had won the power struggle and were supreme in the highlands. After these events Viracocha remained in retirement and Yupanqui was hailed as *Pachacuti* (cataclysm). He retained the leadership and had himself crowned as the Inca ruler.

The Late Inca or Empire period begins with the rule of Pachacuti Inca Yupanqui in 1438 and ends with the Spanish conquest of 1532. The history of this period is much more reliable. Reasonable dates are recorded for the reigns of the Inca rulers and the militaristic expansion of the empire over the whole of the Andean area (*4*).

Pachacuti Inca consolidated previous conquests and new alliances by giving these subjects land near Cuzco, and by allowing them to participate in the new organization of Cuzco with the right to call themselves Incas. He then set about formulating reforms which were to incorporate new provinces into the expanding state. He led a campaign to the lower Urubamba provinces, west through Quechua and Chanca country, and to the southern provinces as far as Lake Titicaca, to subjugate and incorporate these areas into an empire.

After these conquests, due to the pressures of creating an effective administrative government, Pachacuti Inca stayed in Cuzco, leaving his armies under the command of his brother

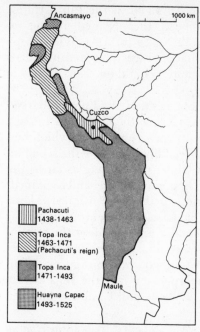

4 *The extent of the Inca Empire showing territory annexed by military campaigns in the Late Inca period* (After Rowe)

Capac Yupanqui, whose orders were to move north making conquests within a clearly defined and limited area, probably as far as Huánuco. Complications arose after a successful campaign when a Chanca contingent, assigned to the army by Pachacuti Inca, deserted near Huánuco. Capac Yupanqui pursued the Chanca past the specified limits, lost them, and, perhaps hoping to regain Pachacuti Inca's favour, attacked and took Cajamarca, the most powerful province in the northern highlands. Leaving a small garrison there, Capac Yupanqui returned to Cuzco, where he was executed for exceeding his orders and for letting the Chanca escape.

The harsh treatment received by Capac Yupanqui is better understood when we look at the situation from Pachacuti Inca's viewpoint. Cajamarca was an important province and had an alliance with the Chimu, an expanding, powerful and extremely well-organized coastal state which was the only real danger to Inca expansion in that direction. Pachacuti was not prepared to meet the full Chimu force at this time and had no wish to provoke them to attack the unprotected garrison left in the prematurely conquered Cajamarca. Also, Capac Yupanqui, due to his apparent success, may have aroused Pachacuti Inca's jealousy.

Pachacuti Inca himself first squashed a revolt in the south, in the Titicaca Basin, before he was able to turn his attention north again. When he did so, *Topa Inca*, his son and heir, was able to head the army and carried out a campaign through the northern highlands as far as Quito. Then, reaching the coast of Ecuador, Topa Inca turned his army south, approached the Chimu from where they were least prepared. He succeeded in subjugating the whole of the north and central coast as far as the Lurin valley. Soon after this vast campaign Topa Inca headed another to subdue the south coast valleys from Nazca to Mala. While Topa Inca expanded the empire, Pachacuti Inca remained in Cuzco organizing the administration and rebuilding Cuzco into a suitable capital for an empire.

Topa Inca became ruler in about 1471. He had just embarked on a campaign in the eastern forest, when the Colla and Lupaca organized an up-rising in the south—a serious threat which had to be dealt with quickly. After successfully squashing the rebellion Topa Inca invaded Bolivia and Chile, penetrating as far as the River Maule, where the southern boundary was set and remained.

After completing the expedition to the eastern forests, Topa Inca remained, like his father, in Cuzco, concentrating on the organization of the empire, extending and adapting the administration's policies towards the many new peoples and provinces of contrasting environments, now unified under one government. It is probable that this Inca incorporated into the Inca system some of the ideas of the Chimu, since he had Chimu nobles and craftsmen brought to live in Cuzco.

Topa Inca died in 1493 and was succeeded by his son *Huayna Capac*. This Inca dealt with some revolts and added new territories to the empire at Chachapoyas and Moyobamba, and north of Quito, where he set the boundary markers on the Ancasmayo river (today the boundary between Ecuador and Colombia). He was also responsible for properly integrating Ecuador into the empire and for building new towns like Tomebamba, where he lived for extended periods. Before he died in Tomebamba, unexpectedly of the pestilence, Huayna Capac learnt that strange bearded men had been seen on the coast (Pizarro's preliminary expedition).

During the five years remaining of the Inca empire, two of Huayna Capac's sons Atahuallpa and Huascar, waged a civil war for the leadership. Atahuallpa was the victor and was preparing for his official coronation just before the Spaniards returned in 1532 (see Chapter 10).

2

The Incas and the people

PHYSICAL APPEARANCE AND GROOMING

The people of the Andean area, like all the other prehistoric inhabitants of America, are called Amerindians, and all show some of the main characteristics of the mongoloid race from which they originated. Most have straight black hair, little body hair, reddish-brown or yellowish-brown skin, and dark brown or black eyes, over which some degree of the epicanthic fold gives the eyes a slanted look but protects them from glare and the cold. Also characteristic of all mongoloid babies is the blueish-purple mark just above and between the buttocks. The variety in the physical appearance of the Andean people is caused partly by differing environmental conditions—for instance, the highland indians are built more powerfully than their coastal contemporaries (5).

The *Inca* had adapted well to the highlands environment. They had broad shoulders and deep chests with lungs whose capacity was expanded to obtain more oxygen from the rarified air of the mountains. While the coastal indians and we ourselves would run the risk of *soroche*, a mountain sickness caused by the lack of oxygen over about 3,000 metres, (over 9,000 ft) elevation, the highland indians had no difficulty in carrying out tasks requiring considerable energy at sea level, including lifting and moving great stones for their building projects. These stocky highlanders were of small to medium height and had very strong, well-developed legs which carried them great distances and enabled them to carry heavy loads. The women, though of slighter build, also showed considerable endurance in carrying heavy loads, often including their latest child slung in a mantle.

The Incas were quite good looking. Atahuallpa Inca was, for

5 Highland indians

instance, described by the Spaniards as having a handsome and elegant appearance. Characteristic facial features of the indians in the Cuzco region today are high cheekbones, broad brows, wide, generous mouths, and slightly pointed chins which give their faces an oval look. Most striking are their fine noses which are often quite prominent and slightly hooked. While bodily hair was slight, facial hair was almost non-existent; beards were quite unknown among the Incas and stray hairs which appeared late in life were plucked with tweezers.

The level of personal hygiene was high among the Incas, but different standards may have corresponded to the position of the individual in the hierarchy. Cleanliness was certainly a virtue practised by the ruling class, but while it was encouraged among the commoners the Spaniards' observations do not suggest that there was a high standard maintained among the latter.

The Inca Emperors bathed often, in sunken baths of closely fitted masonry (7), in the palace grounds. Hot and cold water was brought to these baths in stone channels or copper pipes. Other baths were built where there were natural hot springs and in these the rulers were accustomed to spend several days relaxing from the pressures of government from time to time. Atahuallpa was

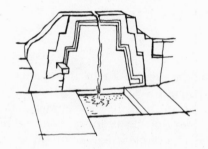

6 *Fountain at Ollantaytambo*

7 *Bath in the palace at Huánuco*

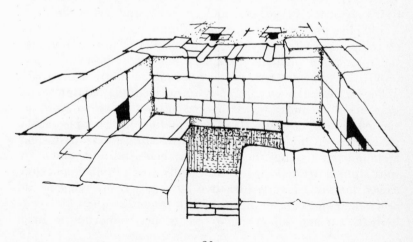

8 Inca woman at her toilet: attendants wash the Coya's hair.
9 grooming

reported to have lodged beside the thermal baths at Cajamarca, while he was awaiting the arrival of the Spaniards there.

Cleanliness was also an important part of worship and many rituals included washing the body, purification, or even public bathing accompanied by a change of clothing. Fountain baths were standard architectural units at many sites in the Cuzco-Urubamba region, where they lined the main thoroughfares or stairways of the sites. These fountains (6), and rivers elsewhere would have provided facilities for maintaining a high standard of cleanliness as well as providing for other general needs. However, the coldness of highland streams would, most probably, have proved a deterrent to any zeal for personal hygiene in many areas.

Personal appearance is, of course, always influenced by fashion, style, and adornment, which in some cultures includes distortions carried out on the body. Head deformation, for example, which has a profound effect on appearance, was used by some coastal and highland indians, but the Incas themselves did not practise it. Inca women are reported to have cultivated plump thighs and calves, considered very attractive by the men, by tying bands below their knees and at the top of their thighs.

Headwear and hairstyling were extremely important in Inca

society and played a vital role in civil life, since the rank and provenance of individuals was recognized mainly by their appearance in this respect. Inca men wore a fringe over their foreheads and a long bob behind, which covered their ears. They probably cut their hair with obsidian knives, rather than the stone knives referred to in the chronicles. However, the women never cut their hair except as a sign of mourning or disgrace. As recorded by Guaman Poma (8, 9) the Inca women wore their hair parted in the middle and falling straight down. They kept their hair clean and shining with frequent washing and combing; and those who liked to keep their hair black and lustrous would dye their hair if it went brown or the ends split. The dyeing process, an ordeal which required precaution against scalding, required a woman to lie on her back placing her hair in a cauldron —in which a mixture of herbs including *chuchan* were boiling. Hairstyles varied throughout the empire. Other styles for men included partly shaving the head, while women might vary theirs by using two braids and sometimes many small braids over their heads. Combs (8) were made of a row of thorns tied between two shivers of wood.

Whereas different hairstyles may not have been compulsory for each province under Inca rule, headdresses certainly were. Except for the *chulla* caps that the Colla wore, there were two main types of headwear. First, the braid to bind the hair was worn by both men and women and could be made of various fabrics, widths and lengths. Secondly, a square cloth folded lenthwise three or four times and laid on the head was used only by Inca women (11). The women's braids were passed around the head only once and tied with braided cords, while the ruler wore a band, just over a finger wide, which was wrapped many times around the head so that it appeared to be about six centimetres in width. Symbols of status and province were added to the braids and supported by them. The ruler wore a series of tassels in the centre of the forehead and a pompon on a short stick above it (10).

The face itself did not receive the more lavish attention that the Aztecs, and some Old World civilizations, seem to have indulged in for sheer coquetry. On the other hand, the chroniclers remarked on the natural colour in the highlander's cheeks. Information on face painting for the Incas is scanty and it is not known whether cosmetics were used for personal adornment. Instead, paint was evidently used on the face for its magical import. During certain festivals and rituals, vermilion from cinnebar and reddish-purple from achiove or genipa was used to paint the face and body; also, warriors may have used this paint before going to war, in order to frighten their enemies. Blood at llama sacrifices was used by the priests to draw lines on the faces of those making the offering. Black was generally the colour of mourning and the women painted their faces black for this purpose.

DRESS

Clothing in the highlands needed to be warm. Inca clothing was made from the wool of the alpaca and vicuña, but with improved communications from the coast, cotton became available and the Inca administrators and colonies in coastal regions naturally adopted this cooler fabric for local wear. Inca clothes were never tailored but were extremely simply made; straight seams of the edges of woven rectangles were sewn together or held at the front with a knot or with straight metal pins.

The commoners and most subject peoples made their own everyday wear, woven with the natural coloured fibres of the alpaca, or of cotton on the coast. While they were restricted in their use of colourful ornamentation by the Incas, the latter made full use of a wide range of gorgeous natural dyes for their clothing. Inca clothing is characterized by its variety of textures, weaves and brilliant colours, used in highly ornate patterns into which gold threads and ornaments might be woven or sewn. The range of colours was carefully and tastefully controlled. Colourful borders or ornate details were used on plainer, one-coloured garments, while the richest and gayest were worn by the ruler and were used for ceremonial and festive wear (*10*). Individuality in dress was not encouraged and for all intents and purposes it was strictly standardized, with slight variations of the regulations, and ornamentation permitted only on a regional or hierarchial basis.

All adult males from the age of puberty, at about 14 years old, wore the basic item of attire which was the loincloth or breechcloth. This was simply a strip of cloth, about 15 centimetres (6 in.) wide, which passed between the legs and was anchored at the front and back over a belt, from which the ends hung down. A sleeveless tunic worn over the breechcloth consisted of a long piece of cloth with a slit in the middle for the head. This cloth hung to just above the knees and was doubled with the sides sewn

10 Male dress; on the right the Inca is shown in a military helmet

up to the armpits, leaving room for the arms. Special types of tunics, including one which was long, were worn for certain special occasions. Fine tunics were decorated in a number of different ways, with a wealth of geometric detail woven into them with good firm colours. The finest tunics were decorated all over (*84*).

The fundamental elements in Inca ornamentation were squares arranged in rows, either plain or filled with constantly recurring little ornaments. A design often worn by the Inca ruler, depicted in numerous drawings by Guaman Poma, consisted of an inverted triangle at the neck and a broad band around the waist of small squares in rows. There were proper names for different shirt designs and these may have had heraldic significance. In the army, shirts of distinctive patterns were worn by different squadrons. Priests too had certain characteristic details displayed in their dress; the high priest wore a long shirt reaching to the ground and over it a second one, covered with ornamentation.

As a rule the coastal male dress varied slightly from that worn by the Incas, a rather shorter shirt was used—which also had sleeves. In some areas shirts reached only to the navel—but the shortest must have been those of the Amazonian tribes who no doubt wore none at all and over whom the Incas had little real influence.

A cloak or mantle was worn over the tunic. This covered only the back and shoulders, but the size varied and sometimes cloaks were large. Two corners of the cloak were usually tied at the front over the chest, or it could be worn with the knot tied at one shoulder leaving that arm free. Certain colours and the degree of ornamentation of the cloak, as with the shirt, varied according to the status of the individual. Under the cloak a small bag for carrying coca leaves was carried slung from the shoulder.

Footwear was similar for both sexes. The Incas usually wore sandals whose soles were made from the neck of the llama. Since the leather was untanned the sandals had to be discarded in wet weather because the sole softened. Wool and aloe-fibre were also used extensively for making sandals, especially those to be worn for festivals and important occasions. The sandals had elaborate fastenings of braided wool cords with a raised pile surface for softness and sandal tops were sometimes decorated with small gold and silver masks. Peculiar to male attire were knee and ankle fringes (*10*).

While all the Andeans within the Inca empire, except for some tribes bordering the selva, had footgear, it varied considerably, so that the Aymara in the south wore mocassin slippers and cotton braids were used on the coast. Apparently the Ecuadorian tribes did not use sandals until these were introduced by the Incas.

Women's clothes were as simply made as the men's and they wore no undergarments. Inca women wore a long sleeveless dress of rectangular cloth, which is nicely described by Cieza in an often quoted passage, which refers to the dress worn by women near Quito.

Some of the women wear the very graceful dress of those of Cuzco, with a long mantle extending from the neck to the feet, leaving the arms free. Round the waist they fasten a very broad and graceful belt called *chumpi*, which tightens and secures the mantle. Over this they wear another fine mantle falling from the shoulders, and coming down so as to cover the feet, called *lliclla*. To secure their mantles they wear pins of gold and silver, rather broad at one end, called *topu*. On the head they wear a very graceful band, which they call *uncha*, and the *usutas*, or sandals complete their attire. In short, the dress of the ladies of Cuzco is the most graceful and rich that has been seen up to this time in all the Indies.

The ends of the dress were drawn up over the shoulders and

fastened with pins so that the arms were free, also, below the waistband the mantle opened to permit movement, showing part of the leg and thigh. The sash was decorated with ornate patterns in squares: It could be broad or narrow and was wound several times around the waist (*11*). The shoulder mantle made of fine wool and often woven in rich patterns, was mainly an outdoor garment. The metal pins that fastened the shoulder mantle were a woman's chief ornament and were made of gold, silver, copper or bronze, according to the status of the wearer. Some of the pins had very large round discs at the top which may have served as mirrors. Another variation of ornament (*11*) shows a *Coya*, Inca queen, with two big pins or discs hanging down covering her breasts, while her attendants have small pins fastening their shoulder mantles.

Both sexes wore jewellery, although it was the men who wore most ornaments among the Incas, since their purpose was to denote rank and status. Most women wore only their pins and necklaces of shell, or bone beads. Flowers also may have been part of a woman's dress since these are often associated with women's dress and women are depicted holding flowers.

The most important symbols of status among the men were the large cylindrical ear-plugs of gold, wood or other material, worn by all men of royal lineage and by those who were called 'Incas by privilege'. These plugs were worn through the ear lobes with the large round end faced forwards. Boys' ears were pierced to receive

11 Female dress

the plugs at the puberty rites, when they also first put on their breechcloths. Metal discs, hung from the neck as breast ornaments, were worn by captains and warriors to whom they were given by the state as awards for bravery in war (33). Wide bracelets of gold and silver were only worn by the highest officials. Small gold masks, already mentioned, were worn occasionally on the sandals, the shoulders, and at the knees. Feathers were also used for ornamentation in headdresses, as collars, or were woven into clothing for special occasions.

PERSONALITY

The emphasis put by the Incas on the pageantry of elaborate public ceremonies, festivals and religious ritual, played an important part in unifying the many cultures and peoples of the empire into a single nation, while at the same time providing opportunities for individuals to indulge in and express sides of their character normally carefully diverted into work activities.

Perhaps it is the seemingly unsurmountable difficulties of the environment that flavour the highland personality with its rather fatalistic outlook. In a land where the mountains tower above one, earthquakes and landslides shake the ground, where a few miles could take all day to walk, and where growth and warmth depend on the generosity of the sun, the fatalistic approach is understandable. Investment in many beliefs and much ceremony becomes an insurance against disaster. Many activities, including those economically necessary such as agriculture, were carefully regulated and accompanied by a wealth of ritual and seasonal festivities.

It is difficult to construct a full-face picture of the Inca personality. The many views put forward of the Incas reveal a range of biases—from cruel and ambitious tyrants to gentle ambassadors of culture. From their works and achievements it is evident that they were certainly able and cunning warriors among whom the virtues of bravery and obedience rated highly. They showed themselves to be impressive organizers with an almost puritanical obsession for work. The art work suggests a fastidiousness combined with an elegance not previously met with in the Andean personality. Yet none of these qualities really provides one with a human insight into the Inca personality. It was their realism and their ability to rationalize their philosophy that was most striking and characteristic.

A mixture of ambition and idealism, combined with a realistic approach to the inherent qualities of the environment, enabled the Incas to bring some economic improvement and security to their subjects, although they achieved this at the expense of individual freedom. One improvement was an assured food supply at all times; another was the general application of a system of agricultural exchange, based on ancient practices, which ensured a more balanced diet for everybody.

FOOD AND DRINK

The basics of the diet were maize, potatoes, and quinua which were stored domestically by everyone between harvests. Additional delicacies such as a little meat, and herbs, could be added to a range of boiled or roasted dishes. There were no fried dishes since ceramic cooking utensils are not suitable for frying. Clay stoves, usually placed inside the houses, were used for cooking. These stoves, about a hand in height, were very economical in their use of fuel; two sticks of wood were slowly fed into a small opening for stoking and pots were placed on two or three round openings on the top of the stove.

Maize was called *murchu* when it was toasted hard, and *capia* when it was boiled and became soft and tasty. Maize flour was ground by women on broad flat stones with the swinging motion of a long half-moon shaped stone which crushed the grain as it was hand rocked from side to side (*12*). A roughly carved or naturally shaped cylindrical stone was used as a pestle to crush smaller amounts of grain and herbs in the hollow of a riverstone,

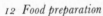

12 Food preparation

13 Mortar bowl and pestle

or some other form of stone bowl (*13*). Maize cakes were made with flour from which the bran had not been sifted. Since making the flour was a time-consuming job these cakes were rarely made for home consumption, and were usually only prepared for special occasions in the form of porridge or dumplings. Small maize cakes and sweet tamales called *huminta* were mainly made as gifts. Popcorn—maize toasted until it splits—was considered a delicacy.

The dishes most commonly cooked were soups and stews made from a variety of ingredients such as maize and many kinds of potatoes—(including *chuño*, dehydrated potato, and *oca*, a sweet potato of various types and colours) and three or four types of beans. In addition oca, a long shaped root, can also be eaten raw (another type, *cavi* became sweet, like jam, after being dried in the sun). *Quinua*, a very nourishing grain, is rich in protein and can be eaten in soups and stews, and the leaves are tender and tasty when cooked. Squashes and bananas imported from the hot lands were sometimes added to the stews. *Ají* (chili pepper) was used in all types of cooking and so were other herbs. *Montepatasca* was a stew made by cooking maize seeds with ají and herbs until the maize seeds split open. *Pisqui*, a stew similar to the former, was enriched and thickened by adding quinua.

Cold-land products like potatoes, chuño, oca, quinua, ulluco, anu, and dried meat could be supplemented with some similar produce from warmer valleys and with maize, a grain called *tarhui*, *molle* (a tree bearing red berries), one type of chili pepper and squash. Hotter lowland products obtained by exchange included maize, manoic, ají, avocados, tomatoes, squashes, beans and lima beans, also peanuts, honey and fruits. Sun-dried preserves were made of bananas and guavas by adding sugar from honey.

The Andean area was rich in nourishing tubers and fruits, but like the rest of Pre-Columbian America, lacked the large domestic animals which provided the Old World with a generous meat supply. The indians, who were not vegetarians by choice, only rarely ate meat and then usually at banquets and festivals. Jerked meat was more often available. This was preserved, dried without salt by cutting the meat into thin strips and exposing it to the sun and frost. It was then pounded and thinned out between two stones. One dish made with jerked and fresh meat, ají, chuño, potatoes, and other vegetables was called *locro*, and a similar stew was made with fish which could be dried. Although salt was not used in the meat-drying process, it was used in cooking and was obtained from the saline rivers and lakes, from which it was recovered by evaporation.

Llama meat is tender and tastes like mutton or, in the case of a four-or five-month-old animal, like lamb. However, like the alpaca and vicuña, it had other uses and could not be eaten indiscriminately. The only regular meat supply available to the indians was the guinea pig, which is delicious when roasted. These animals multiplied quickly in indian kitchens or houses, and were fed on food scraps and green plants (*69*). Some kinds of ducks were domesticated but little is known about how they were kept or who ate them. Fishing was important in some regions, around Lake Titicaca and on the coast, but did not play an important role in the diet of most highland areas. The Inca Emperor himself enjoyed a fresh supply of fish brought by runners from the coast.

In most regions all game was preserved for seasonal hunts organized by the Inca officials to increase the meat supply. Among edible wild game there were two kinds of deer, *Loyco* and *Taroka*, the guanaco and also the viscacha. Rabbits, partridges, waterfowl and small birds were also eaten. The Incas however, did not eat dog meat and they despised the Huanca, who did. In some parts of Ecuador and in the jungle, the Incas encountered tribes who practised cannibalism. This they considered very barbaric and tried to stamp it out.

One Spanish historian, Cobo, is most derisive in his description of indian cooking habits. He considers their stomachs were amazingly strong to hold the quantity and quality of food they consumed—'coarse foods eaten almost raw . . . and digested quickly'. Description of receptions at the Inca court, however, suggest a much more sophisticated attitude to food preparation, and perhaps a generally higher standard during the Inca period.

14 Metal cups: a silver kero from Cuzco, 8 cms high
15 A gold effigy face beaker from the North Coast, 12¼ cms high

The nobility, administrators and the important curaca had their food served to them on gold and silver dishes, which were shaped in imitation of the pottery ones used by the commoners (*16*). Similarly, the shape of large drinking mugs called *qero* or *kero*, made of wood or pottery, which were used by the indians, were imitated in metals for the élite (*14, 15*). Cooking utensils were made of pottery in the shapes illustrated in (*16*). Inca cooking pots had covers and some had pedestal or tripod bases, so that a fire could be built around them. Additional kitchen utensils included wooden ladles, bone skewers and a copper or bronze semi-lunar knife called *tumi* (*76*).

Everyone ate twice a day, at about eight or nine o'clock in the morning, and again at an hour or two before sunset. There was no need for furniture, the table was the ground and while the élite, persons of prestige and the curaca used cloths on which the food and dishes might be placed, the commoners often did not bother. The men and women ate together sitting back to back on the ground and using each others' shoulders for mutual support. The woman served the soups and stews in dishes from ceramic ollas and got up to fill her husband's plate or get him a drink when he wanted it. Pachacuti, the ninth Inca, ordered that everyone should eat outside in their patios, and at festivals the entire population of a village should eat in the curaca's patio, where he as the local chief headed the 'table' seated on his *duho* (a low stool). Banquets lasted most of the day and often several days in sucession. Food was brought by each household and was shared. Drink was also supplied but at the individual's own expense.

On these occasions each group sat in the position they occupied in relation to others in the social organization. The principal division was between *Hanansaya* on one side and *Hurinsaya* on the other side of the curaca, so that the two moieties (each being half of the total community) sat facing each other in two parallel lines. It was customary for a man from one side to carry across two cups of *chicha*, to offer one to a member of the other side, and then drink the second cup himself. This formality was enacted also at meetings of the Emperor with his officials and the curacas, and was a standard ritual at all social occasions. Alliances could be sealed by this drinking ritual and each side would keep the cup from which they drank, to remind them of their commitment.

Chicha was the native word for fermented drinks which were made from several types of cultivated plants: maize, quinua, oca and also from molleberries. Great quantities of chicha were consumed during festivals, but it was also drunk every day at varying strengths and was the only drink kept by the Andeans in their houses. The chicha was made by a time-consuming process in which the women chewed the pulp of the fruit used and spat

16 Ceramic domestic utensils: the three smaller vessels were used for serving food; the central jar for storage; the pedestal bowl and brazier for cooking

it out into jars of warm water. Cloudy water was preferred since good clear water was considered to make sour chicha. Chicha made of maize was tastier than that made with quinua, but the strongest chicha was made from molleberries, which could also be used to top up and improve the maize chicha. The molleberries could be boiled to make a rich syrup.

Vinupa was a very strong drink made of toasted maize, which was steeped until it began to sprout and then ground and boiled in water. Once strained, the drink was kept until it fermented. It was however, forbidden for general use, and, like the stimulant *coca*, was used mainly in religious rituals.

LANGUAGE AND LITERATURE

The numerous small political units which the Incas united under their rule may have spoken nearly as many languages and dialects. Linguistic diversity was permitted to continue under the Inca regime, but they also introduced *Quechua*, after 1438, for general use.

Quechua or 'Quichua' is an inappropriate name for the language of the Incas since it was taken from the Andean province of this name with the same language. The accepted explanation is that the Incas superimposed their own original tongue on others for the administration of their empire—which presupposes that Quechua was similar or closely related to their own language. However, there is an interesting reference to an alternative possibility: Cobo records that the Incas once spoke a special language which was used only by the nobility. Topa Atau, Huayna Capac's nephew, who lived until 1580, affirmed this and said that they had forgotten the language since so many Incas were killed in the civil and Spanish wars. Since elsewhere Quechua is also referred to as the 'general' language of Cuzco, the only possible explanation would be that the Incas once had another language, before they settled in the Cuzco region.

Quechua was used for the purposes of government and for inter-communication between all the provinces. Many Andeans became bilingual and all were expected to teach their children Quechua from an early age. The introduction of Quechua-speaking *mitimaes* (colonists) into foreign districts (p. 109) was one of their most efficient methods of spreading the use of the language.

Quechua is easy to learn and speak, and is similar to Latin languages in that it has the eight figures of speech (nouns, pronouns, verbs etc.), but there are no articles and no genders added to nouns. The plural of nouns and some pronouns, and of the verbs, is formed by adding the particle *cuna*, eg. *runa* (man)— *runacuna* (men). Adjectives are placed before the substantives and genders are only expressed by adding the words *ccari* (man), and *huarmi* (woman), or *urco* (male) or *china* (female), for animals. When these words are not added to the nouns they are common. Possessive pronouns are formed by affixes added to the nouns. Most adjectives of quality, likeness, or comparison become adverbs by adding *hina* or *sina: sinchi* (strong)—*sinchi-hina* (powerfully).

The language does not have a large vocabulary, but words can vary in their meaning by their location in a sentence, or by a slight change of accent and pronunciation. The extensive use of nominal and verbal particles to alter the parts of speech and modify meaning gives the language a great power of expression and flexibility. Words could be adopted from other languages by using existing elements in the Quechua language to make up new words.

Although the Incas did not have writing, they were able to preserve a wealth of detailed information by the use of a system of knotted and coloured cords, called *quipu(s)*. These consisted of a main cord from which coloured woollen threads hung. The position and number of knots tied on these threads provided numerical information based on the decimal system (*17*). The *quipucamayoc(s)* (keepers of the quipus) were only able to decipher or interpret those quipus which had been explained to them.

Although used mainly for administrative and statistical information, quipus could also be used as aids in recording historical and liturgical information accumulated by the government. The idea that a bunch of quipus could be read like a book is fictitious, but in the hands of the professional quipucamayocs, who were trained in their use and in memorized histories, traditions and literature, these instruments were such useful memory aids that it might well have been assumed that they were actually being read like braille.

Another aid to memory was in the form of painted boards, kept in the Coricancha, the principal temple of the Incas. These were ordered by Pachacuti Inca, to depict the history of his ancestors, but must have been added to by subsequent Incas.

Inca 'literature' was oral and was passed on from generation to

17 Quipus, knotted cords used for accounting and to record mainly statistical information

generation. Only fragments of recitations were written down as literature at the time of the conquest, although more of their content survived in some of the Spanish accounts written largely from these sources. Surviving pieces take the form of prayers, hymns, narrative poems and dramas, love poems and songs. The qualities for which they are noted are those of clarity and beauty of expression and feeling, accompanied by a rigid phonetic pattern which gives a rhythmical character impressive in oral recitation.

The narrative poems were sung or recited at public occasions: 'at such times those who knew the ballads, with loud voice, their eyes on the Inca, sang to him of what his forebears had done'. Many of these narratives 'differed on many points' but were generally concerned with historical events and the reigns of the Incas, whose praises they naturally sang. However, if an Inca was not popular such narratives were suppressed and his name was only mentioned in the genealogies. This may have been the case with Inca Urcon, who was Pachacuti's cowardly brother. According to some accounts Viracocha Inca retired to let Urcon take over as Inca, but when the latter failed to protect Cuzco from the advancing Chanca army, he was usurped by Pachacuti Inca. As a result, Urcon was hardly mentioned in the oral histories.

It was the duty of the chiefs and heads of lineages to preserve the memory and history of their ancestors. One verse from a narrative piece on the death of Pachacuti Inca survives in a recording from Sarmiento:

I was born like a lily in the garden,
And so also was I brought up.
As my age came, I have grown up,
And, as I had to die, so I dried up,
       And I died.

Another extract, below, is very straightforward and rhythmic taken from Pachacuti Yamqui's chronicle. In this piece, Chuchicapac of the Hatuncollas (Titicaca area) came to the marriage of Viracocha Inca, bringing with him all his guard, his retinue and his precious ancestral idol. He was probably seeking to enlist the Inca's aid against his rivals the Lupaca. He repeated many times to the Inca:

Cam Cuzcocapaca,	You are king of Cuzco,
Nuca Collcapaca,	I am king of Colla,
Upiasun	We will drink
Micusun	We will eat
Rimasun	We will speak
Amapi rima (chun)	Of what no-one else has spoken.
Nuca collque tiyacani	I am rich in silver
Chuqui tiyacani	I am rich in gold
Viracocha Pachayachic	Viracocha, symbol of the universe,
Mucha	I adore,
Nucac inti muchac.	The sun I adore.

Pachacuti Inca is considered to have been responsible for reorganizing Inca history and traditions into an acceptable form at a time when the empire was expanding, in order to impress and present Inca credentials to a wider public. A more abstract expression of traditional ideas may be incorporated in the narrative myths and legends. A number of origin myths set out to explain Inca religion, moral codes and customs. Some of these myths were probably devised by the *amautas* (wise men) to account for older local legends and beliefs, in order to satisfy subject provinces of their validity! Among the Inca origin myths, of

47

which there are several different versions, one describes Viracocha as the Creator, populating the world from Titicaca—and the birth of Manco Capac from the water of the lake. This version of the myth should have satisfied those subjects who lived in the Titicaca basin, like the Collas—while providing the Incas with a more impressive genealogy linking up their Sun God to the Creator.

Garcilaso tells us that the amautas composed comedies and dramas 'for performance at court, before the kings and lords on solemn feast days'. The plays were treated very seriously and in Cuzco, the actors, who were members of the élite, were from all the professions. Valuable gifts and jewels were given to those actors who gave good performances. So powerful were the feelings and traditions preserved in these plays that the Peruvian government passed a decree in 1781, forbidding the indians to enact dramas with themes concerning their ancestors. Garcilaso says that lofty prose was used in the dramas and that they were about heroic exploits and wars, as well as the histories and greatness of the past Inca rulers. The comedies, on the other hand, were concerned with agriculture, property, family and household themes. Garcilaso also tells us how the plays were memorized by the actors: 'they repeat each word many times, marking it with

18 Musicians playing wind and percussion instruments

a coloured pebble, pip, seed or chuy beans. Thus they remember the words easily.' The plays were accompanied by music played on flutes and drums (*18*), the main Andean instruments (p. 50), and, on occasions, by dancing.

Only in rare instances have examples of Inca folklore survived. One such example was copied by Garcilaso from Padre Blas Valera's papers, and he records it as follows:

Sumac ñusta	Fair princess
Torallaiquim	Your brother
Puinuyquita	Your urn
Paquircayan	Now breaks
Hina mantara	Causing the
Cunununun	Brilliant explosions
Illapantac	Of thunderbolts falling
Camri ñusta	But you, royal maiden
Unuiquita	Their clean waters
Para munqui	Give us in rain
Mai nimpiri	And sometimes
Chichi munqui	You give us hail
Riti munqui	You give us snow.
Pacharurac	Universal Creator
Pachacamac	Pachacamac
Viracocha	Viracocha
Cai hinapac	For this office
Churasunqui	Appointed you
Camasunqui	Created you.

Another folktale was recorded in about 1750 by Fray Martin de Murúa, which he called 'Inca fairytale of a Famous Shepherd named Acoya-napa, and the Beautiful Chuqui-llantu, Daughter of the Sun'. The Sun's virgins were strictly segregated and this charming love story is filled with the nostalgic yearnings for requited but forbidden love, a theme which recurs frequently in Inca verse, as for instance in the famous, but later, Drama of Ollantay.

Inca poetry was carefully constructed with measured syllables and even the occasional rhyming ends to lines, although it usually consisted of blank verse. In the poems, again love played an important part. A few are happy and gay, but most are sad and nostalgic; the poems are often rich in allusions to nature and environment. Meters were used for the love songs and these were composed with short lines so that they could more easily be played on the flute:

Caylli llapi	In this place
Pununqui	Thou shalt sleep
Chaupituta	Midnight
Samusac	I will come.

The words to musical compositions, songs, chanted verses, were well known and the tunes were played on various types of flute.

MUSIC AND DANCE

Although almost no musical instruments have survived from the Cuzco region, examples elsewhere and historical references are mainly of flutes and percussion instruments. The *quena* flute was made of a joint of cane, open at both ends with a notch at the edge against which the air current is directed. It had a varying number of finger stops, sometimes as many as eight, and was the only instrument widely used among the Andeans. Another wind instrument, panpipes, consisted of several points of cane, or other materials, of graded length tied together. While flutes are not generally suitable for playing war tunes, one type, somewhat larger and made of bone, was used for this purpose. Whistles, producing only one note, were common.

The indians were trained to practise their skill on the flutes to provide music for the Inca court. They played simple tunes and did not attempt to harmonize in unison; instead several pipes could extend the range of notes. Garcilaso suggests that indian voices were not well trained for complicated part singing either, and it is probable that 'chanting' was the most used form of singing.

Pototo, a trumpet made of a large conch (sea shell), played only a single note which carried far and was used for communication and as a signal in time of war—rather like a bugle. Gourd and wooden trumpets have been found on the coast, as have trumpets of copper and silver; these had no variation of tone gained through stops, instead different pitches were used. Big drums were played mainly in war and some of these, especially those used in triumphal marches, were made from the skins of the enemy warriors taken in battle. Drums, whose decoration consisted of gold and silver ornament set with precious stones, were used for important religious ceremonies and occasions. These drums are described as being played before a 'theatre with tiers' erected in the centre of the main plaza. Small drums or tamborines (drums with two membranes held together by a strap in one hand and played with a single stick wound around with many coloured threads), and small copper, bronze and silver bells were used in festivals. Bells varied: bivalve bells consisted of two connected pieces of convex round metalplate and a hole pierced for suspension of the clanger; hawkbells may have been tied on sticks. Jingle rattles of snail shells and coloured beans were used for anklets in dances and may also have been shaken in containers.

Dances were an integral part of most important ceremonies, including public worship. Dancers were dressed in elaborate costumes and took up positions in traditional and easily recognized formations. Outside Cuzco the costumes and dances varied from province to province. The list of Inca dances below is a summarized version of those described in the records, following Rowe:

Taqui	Ritual dance with singing accompanied by four large drums, beaten by indians of high class.
Guacon	Dance for men only.
Guayayturilla	Dance for both sexes to notes played by a guanaco skull pipe.
Haylyc	Farmer's dance.
Cachua	Warrior's dance for both sexes, in which a circle of hands was formed.
Huay-yaya	Special dance of the Inca family, led by men carrying the royal standard.
Campi	Dance accompanied by a great drum, which was carried on the back of an indian of low birth, while a woman beat it.

GAMES AND SPORTS

Organized games were also interwoven with ceremony and public occasions. Ritual games probably existed between community moieties, but sports were encouraged most among the Inca élite. Athletic contests were held every year for the boys' maturity rites. In these, the athletics and team games were devised to test a boy's endurance and prowess for the more serious battles he might be required to fight in the future. Foot-

19 & 20 Carved stones such as these may have been used as gaming boards; however there is also a possibility that they are architectural plans

races, skill in throwing and mock battles were included in these games. The commoners, who were encouraged to express themselves in the competitive activity of manual labour, probably needed some encouragement to exert themselves further! This was, however, provided by the more relaxed sport of feasting and dancing at the festivals, where they were able to enjoy using up their remaining energy in placating the gods and in celebrations.

Royal hunts were organized partly as an entertainment and partly for economic reasons. On these occasions many thousands of indians were ordered to enclose an area of preserve and, shouting loudly, they advanced towards its centre beating the vegetation. When their hands could be joined the animals were penned in and the Inca ruler, or governor in charge, would watch while the male animals were caught and killed with *bolas* (p. 103) and clubs. Afterwards the Inca or his representatives feasted and distributed the fresh meat among those present, the rest was dried and prepared for the Inca Emperor's storehouses. Huayna Capac, the eleventh Inca, in particular seems to have been a very keen sportsman who enjoyed hunting and fishing in his spare time.

General amusements and play were not normally considered important or encouraged for children, as we might expect them to have been. This was due to the highly organized work orientation of society in which even children were expected to occupy themselves usefully, helping their parents and learning various tasks. There were, however, a few simple toys and games. *Pisqoynyo* was a top which was spun by whipping it with a lash (*43*). *Papa Auqui* 'potato chief' and *taucca-taucca* were names of two other games played by the children. Other games, such as those of throwing counters were probably more generally played.

There were a number of games in which dice were used. The dice, *Picqana*, were marked with one to five points and may have been made of ceramic or wood. Hard, inedible chuy beans of different colours with comic names were used, both for keeping scores and for playing games (*19*, *20*). In one such game, movements of the beans were controlled by the throw of the dice. The Incas gambled on these games for amusement, exchanging clothes, and animals as part of the fun. The tenth Inca, Topa Inca Yupanqui, seems to have been something of a gambler. On one occasion he accepted a challenge from his favourite son, to play a dice throwing game called *ayllos*, introduced from the Collao, and he agreed to give his son one of his provinces if he should win. The game was watched by worried spectators who feared the Inca's behaviour if he should lose. However, the Inca ruler did lose and eventually he gave his son the governorship of the province of his choice—Urcosuyu. Henceforth those who inhabited this province were called the Aylluscas in memory of the story. Although this story illustrates well the gambling amusements of this Inca, it should not be overlooked that it may also have a deeper, more abstract significance, used to describe the origin of the ayllos or the aylluscas.

21 Pisqoynyo, *top*

3

The Inca and the
organization of the empire

The Inca Empire was divided into four great provinces or *suyu*
(quarters) called Chinchaysuyu (NW), Antisuyu (NE), Cuntisuyu
(SW), and Collasuyu (SE), whose position was reflected in the plan
of Cuzco, located ideologically at the centre. The Incas called
the empire *Tahuantinsuyu*, meaning the 'Land of the Four
Quarters'. These quarters were subdivided into smaller provinces,
some of which correspond approximately to their pre-Inca native
boundaries, others were re-divided or adjusted in size. Also,
some groups of population in the provinces were removed to,
or exchanged with, those of other parts of the empire under the
Inca system of mitimaes (p.109).

SOCIAL ORGANIZATION
The Inca empire was made up of a structure of small related
local groups, each with its own ancestor cult, which were integrated into larger organizational units. Inca social organization
was strictly hierarchical and relationships in the family and
civil life were very clearly defined, so that no individual, family,
or large group failed to understand their role within their province
or within the empire in any given circumstances.

The *ayllu* is a general indian term used to describe the basic
Andean social (kin/community) and organizational group. The
chroniclers describe the ayllu as a related group of kinsmen or a
lineage descended from a common ancestor. While members of an
ayllu were always normally interrelated in pre-Inca times, under
Inca government it was sometimes necessary to create new
localized groups unrelated to the kinship system; these were
formed for administrative reasons.

In each area of the empire everyone had certain roles or

duties to fulfil; responsibilities varied according to rank and status but these were either political, military or economic, or were connected with ceremonial and ritual. At the top of the hierarchical, social and administrative pyramid came the Inca royal family—an élitist nobility inhabiting the capital of Cuzco and headed by the Inca Emperor.

THE INCAS

The Inca rulers claimed direct descent from the Sun through their ancestor Manco Capac, and therefore, as the Sun's representative on earth, the Emperors ruled by divine right. The power of the ruler was absolute: in theory the *Sapa Inca* (Unique Inca) considered all the men in his empire as his sons and all the women as his spouses. His control over such an extensive territory could however, only be insured by effective government, good military organization and by maintaining some degree of contentment among his subjects. His government was indeed so effective that he had virtually unlimited control over his subjects in what must be one of the most autocratic governments ever implemented.

The nobles of royal blood and 'Incas by privilege' made up the élitist nobility which was the instrument through which the Inca governed. Those of both groups belong to the Inca class and were entitled to wear varied editions of the headband and the large ear-plugs which were worn by the Sapa Inca himself. These large ear-plugs caused them to be given the nickname of 'Orejones' (Big-ears) by the Spanish chroniclers.

22   The headdresses worn by the Emperor and officials denoted rank and provenance

The nobles of royal blood were members of an hereditary aristocracy, descended from the Inca rulers since the legendary founder, Manco Capac. These formed prestigious lineage groups called *panaca*, each of which were made up of all descendants of a ruler in the male line. 'Incas by privilege' on the other hand were not Incas by birth, although some of them were related through political marriages and alliances to the Inca rulers prior to Pachacuti Inca. The main reason for extending privileges to these tribes who lived in the region of Cuzco between Quiquijana, in the Vilcanota valley, and Abancay, was that they were Quechua-speaking allies. With the rapid expansion of the small Inca state into an empire, which took place during Pachacuti Inca's reign in an area which extended from Bolivia to Quito, thousands of trained officials were needed. In the early days of the empire, therefore, anyone who showed any administrative ability, no matter what his background, was a likely candidate for enforcing the Inca government policies in a newly conquered village. Many groups of these 'Incas by privilege' were removed to distant parts of the empire among restless natives—to whom they were supposed to set an example, in addition to indoctrinating them in Inca culture. However, not all of them were transferred in this manner, for Pachacuti Inca had promised, when they came to his aid during the Chanca war, that they would be represented by a place in the organization of Cuzco. Those that remained were formed into ten *ayllu* (organizational kin groups); each of the two main divisions in the organization of Cuzco (*Hanan Cuzco* and *Hurin Cuzco*), having five ayllu.

This bipartite divison into *Hanan* and *Hurin*, was evidently a traditional early and pre-Inca concept of social organization, and was described by the chroniclers as meaning 'upper' and 'lower' respectively. There are two views of the origin of this organization of Cuzco. The first depicts the early Inca occupants living in Hurin Cuzco and expanding later into Hanan Cuzco, so that the ten royal panaca, like the ten ayllu, were integrated into the organization of Cuzco as they were formed. Each Inca ruler founded his own panaca, Inca Roca being the first to rule from Hanan Cuzco. The other view is put forward by Zuidema, who visualizes a simultaneous origin of all the panaca woven into the fabric of the Inca concepts of organization.

The principle of 'quinquepartition' (units of 5 which could easily be doubled to 10 and subsequently to decimalization) was a very important element in the organization of the Inca dynasty, after its contact with the Chimu kingdom. Zuidema notes that only the first ten of the twelve Inca rulers were represented in the organization of Cuzco. Five of these belonged to Hanan Cuzco and five to Hurin Cuzco. He considers therefore, that the Hanan —Hurin relationship can be interpreted as one of kinship relationships to the Inca, Pachacuti Inca, who was responsible for the re-organization of Cuzco. Those in Hanan Cuzco were the primary kin of Pachacuti Inca, and the earlier rulers' descendants became the subsidiary sons in Hurin Cuzco. In this theoretical view of the organization, the ruler would always belong to Hanan Cuzco, and his more distant relatives, illegitimate brothers and subsidiary sons, would belong to Hurin Cuzco.

Zuidema also sees a basic principle of organization based on a division of society into three groups:

Collana	Primary (legal) kin of Inca	Aristocratic rulers
Payan	Subsidiary kin of Inca	Assistants and servants
Cayao	Humanity not related to Collana	Non-aristocratic population

Furthermore, Zuidema finds that these three groups can be extended into a principle of 'quadripartition', which provides a framework for marriage relationships, in which the Hanan and Hurin divisions may also have functioned.

In theory these ideas were applied throughout the Inca empire, but the emphasis in their application reflected the local traditions encountered, which the Incas were at pains to integrate.

THE CURACA

In keeping with their method of superimposing their ideology on the local traditions and practices, the Incas permitted the conquered to be ruled by a member of a leading local family, their native *Sinchi* or chief. Under the Incas they were called *Curaca* and the post was made hereditary, as were most of the other administrative posts, once they were set up. This curaca class was a secondary nobility which enjoyed some of the privileges of the Incas, but those that belonged to it were never given the right to call themselves Incas. While the Incas filled the most responsible positions in the Inca governments, the curaca were in charge of the administration of local populations of approximately 100 taxpayers and over.

THE 'COMMONERS' OR SUBJECT PEOPLES

The real load of the economy was on the shoulders of the rest of the population, the commoners: taxpayers, whose working energy provided the produce and goods on which the administration was supported. For an individual male householder this tax, or tribute payment, was calculated in work performed rather than in goods, as each province was responsible for supplying specified amounts of tribute, in food and goods, to the Inca Emperor's (government) storehouses. Individual taxpayers were accordingly organized to provide the quantities required. The government, in return, was careful to adjust demands to the capacity of the province. Most commoners were peasant farmers who not only cultivated the lands of the Emperor, the produce of which fed the Incas, curacas, and everyone in the service of the empire, but they also laboured on the lands of the Sun and other religions. The produce from these lands was for the support of the priesthood, attendants of the shrines; an enormous amount was also consumed in sacrifices to the idols. In addition, the individual taxpayers might be called upon to fulfil local obligations such as repairing bridges, serving in highway lodgings, as well as being prepared to serve in one of the three main services—the army, the public works force, or the mines.

While the majority of commoners were agriculturists who paid their yearly contributions of work in kind, others received their keep and paid their tax by working at a trade. Where this involved the specialized production of luxury goods requiring tools and materials, the workers lived in the towns, and were supported by those members of the Inca, or curaca class, who could afford them and were licensed to keep them. Others, less specialized, either retained enough land to feed themselves (and their families), or were given supplies while they produced tribute goods in their own houses. In any case, the individual had little time or opportunity for private enterprise. Even the religious, public ritual entertainments and celebrations were organized by the government.

LAW

Incentive for individual enterprise, or ambition to possess luxury goods, were greatly discouraged for commoners by laws concerning private property. No commoner was allowed to possess luxury goods, a category which included any goods in excess of his and his family's immediate material needs, unless he was especially licensed to possess them by the Inca Emperor. Luxury goods were treated as rewards for service. This law prevented crimes relating to property, simply for lack of motivation.

Inca laws were recorded on the quipus for reference like other administrative information, such as the census, tribute accounting, stock-taking and labour availability. There were many laws which came under the following headings: Municipal law, concerning tribal rights; Agrarian laws, dealing with divisions of land; Common law, for collective labour in public works, and the Law of Brotherhood, which maintained collective cooperative work in agriculture; in addition to these there was *Mitachanacuy*, a law governing the distribution of work by turns, or by households, so that all work was meted out fairly to everyone. The Domestic laws required that everyone, whether young or old, should be given tasks, and covered the possession of goods, the providing of inspectors to visit everyone's home to inspect their living standards and levels of hygiene. A Poor law provided the aged and disabled with the necessities of life from the Inca Emperor's storehouses; similarly all travellers on official business were provided for by laws concerning lodgings and supplies, which were free of charge.

Other, Moral laws and rulings were observed individually or were communally based. The punishments given for breaching these were well known and carefully listed and explained (see below).

ADMINISTRATION

Laws were enforced by Inca government administrators and officials (*23*). The level at which a crime or offence was dealt with depended on the nature and importance of the crime committed. The local curaca were not fully empowered to deal with criminals, and serious offences had to be referred to the Inca magistrates and governors in the provincial capitals. Only the Inca governor of a province had the power to order a death sentence carried out. Pachacuti Inca was reported to have said that any judge who permitted himself to be bribed should be regarded as a thief and, as such, punished with death.

For many crimes, some of which would appear to us to be comparatively inoffensive, the punishment meted out under Inca rule was severe: the death sentence was often pronounced and executed for apparently quite petty crimes. This provided a

*23 Inca officials: (*from left to right) *a provincial governor, one of his administrative aids and a quipucamayoc*

strong deterrent to all types of crime and life was only tolerable as a good, obedient citizen. There seems, however, to have been considerable difference between the standard upheld for the commoners and those of the nobility: the latter were not nearly as severely punished as the former. In a case where a commoner would almost certainly receive a death sentence, on a similar charge a member of the Inca class would probably lose face with a public admonishment, or at worst lose some of his public status or privileges; a curaca on the other hand, might risk losing his job. The life of a member of the élite was only threatened when he was labelled a traitor or in some way caused the Inca Emperor's displeasure.

The élite and their sons, which included the governors, captains, curacas, and judges, as well as quipucamayocs (see p 45), architects and engineers, enjoyed certain immunities and tax exemptions. They were supposed to acknowledge the Emperor by gifts made to him whenever they saw him officially. In return, they received 'salaries' in the form of 'gifts' from the Emperor, and rights to receive tribute from the commoners under their jurisdiction, 'given' to them as service. This form of reciprocation which existed between all groups in Inca society was basic to Inca economic organization and created the means whereby goods could be redistributed. The principle of reciprocity was traditional between the community and its leaders; the Incas extended it to include the government and its subjects.

In administrative government the rank of an official depended on the territorial unit and population he was responsible for (*24*): the *Sapa Inca* was the supreme head of government, religion and the army. The four *Apu*(s) (Prefects) held the highest posts under the Sapa Inca, and formed the Inca's Supreme Council. Each Apu represented a *suyu* (quarter) of the empire. Although they were chosen from the highest nobility, usually close relatives of the Emperor, their posts were not hereditary. The *Tocricoc Apu*, Imperial governors who resided in the provincial capitals, had judicial and administrative responsibilities. They were nobles, sometimes closely related to the Emperor, and ruled over populations of about 40,000 taxpayers or householders. The governors were supposed to attend rigorously to two things. 'The first, that they and their subjects should observe and fulfil perfectly the Emperor's laws. The second, that they should consider with great vigilance and care the common and particular interests of their province.' In each province there were many grades of curaca, the native rulers of provinces or villages, whose rank was assessed by the number of taxpayers he had under his authority—which could number between 10,000 and 100 adult men and their families. The taxpayers were organized into groups approximated in a decimal system, as in the diagram (p. 6). The *camayoc* (district leaders) were foremen appointed by their curaca to whom they were responsible; their posts were not hereditary. In addition to these administrative posts, there were those in the other professions and services. The quipucamayocs and perhaps the priests, and those with positions of responsibility in the army and public works force, were structured on parallel lines to those in governmental posts, with seniority ranked according to the number of individuals an official or captain had under his orders. In the provinces, quipucamayocs were responsible only to the Tocricoc Apus, and occupied positions in large and small towns and villages. Inspectors travelled around the provinces, inspecting different aspects of the economy and administration, also private citizens. Chief inspectors organized visitations to assess the tribute capacities of the provinces, and four of these were sent to each of the great suyu, every year or so, to make a report on their findings. The efficiency of the Inca system stirred the admiration of the Spanish chroniclers, and unfortunately aided the conquistadores in their conquest.

Outside this clear hierarchical structure lie two groups: the *Aclla*, Sun Virgins, who are dealt with in the chapter on Religious Life; and the *Yana*. The origin and position of the Yana are difficult to understand since the many brief references to them in the chronicles appear contradictory, or at least confusing. They are usually referred to as perpetual and hereditary servants of the Inca or the Sun, for whom they worked at varied tasks, and, as such, could become quite privileged members of society. The Yana may have started as underprivileged servants, punished for the misconduct of their villages or ethnic group by the loss of their original land rights. By the time of the Spanish conquest they were a class which was expanding into numerous and varied positions in the society. Generally their social position might be equivalent to that of artisans.

THE INCA AND THE ROYAL FAMILY

The titles of the Inca Emperor:

Capac Apu	Emperor, rich and powerful in war
Sapa Inca	Unique Inca
Intip Cori	Son of the Sun
Capac Titu	Liberal and powerful Lord
Huacchacuyac	Lover and bene-factor of the poor

The titles of the Inca Empress:

Coya	Empress, Queen
Mamanchic	Our Mother

The titles of the royal children:

Auqui	Prince
Ñusta	Princess

24 Royal titles

Inca meant Emperor, and referred to the royal ruler himself, but it was also a title used by all his descendants in the male line, meaning a man of royal blood. This title, and that of *Intip Churin* (Child of the Sun), could also be used for male members of the royal family who showed some distinction, usually in the religious field. Unmarried sons of the Inca were called *Auqui*, and *Inca* when they were married. Similarly the unmarried daughters were called *Ñusta* and then *Palla* (women of royal blood) when they married. The illegitimate daughters were called Ñusta, with the name of their mothers' province before it, for example Colla Ñusta. Neither the curacas, however important they were, nor their wives or children could take these names which were used solely by the Inca royal family. While the 'Incas by privilege' called themselves Inca their wives and daughters could not call themselves Palla like those of royal blood 'since women, incapable of bearing arms in war like men, were also incapable of bearing that royal name'! The Emperor sometimes gave female relatives of bastard birth to a great curaca or other subjects deserving outstanding recognition, but the children of such a union were called after the father and the woman lost her title of Palla.

The kin terms were absolute, ranked from the point of reference of the living Emperor, so that the rank of sons (legitimate and illegitimate) were distinguished by him in different kin terms, for descendants down to great-great-grandchildren. The bastard sons were relegated to different generations of descent, the lowest of which was 'nephew'. The terms also denote the degree of closeness to the ancestor figure when the Inca ruler died.

When an Inca Emperor died, either his eldest legitimate son, or the most suitable of his legitimate sons, inherited his titles. All the other sons founded together a *panaca*, a lineage group of which the deceased Inca became the ancestor figure. The word 'panaca' expresses the unity of a descent group forged at its head, by the union of a brother and sister, whose members inherited the palace and estates of the deceased Emperor.

Legitimate sons were the offspring of the marriage of the Emperor with his principal wife. The early Inca rulers married into other tribes in the Cuzco region, forming alliances with the outside world in order to strengthen their position and authority. Pachacuti Inca Yupanqui was the first Inca ruler to marry his full sister and this formed a precedent which was closely followed by his successors. The custom was expressed in the origin accounts, in which Manco Capac was portrayed as forming the Inca line by marrying his sister. The practice of marrying a full sister was permitted only for the Emperor, in order to ensure that the royal children born of his principal wife guaranteed the royal descent, keeping the royal blood pure (at least by 50 percent should the Coya have conceived elsewhere). If the Coya proved to be barren, the Emperor could only marry, as his principal wife, another sister, or his nearest living female relative, such as a first cousin.

The Emperor kept many other wives or concubines who bore him illegitimate children but these could not inherit the Incaship under any circumstances. The number of these secondary wives reached into the hundreds and it is easy to perceive that with the number of illegitimate children born to an Inca ruler, it was essential to make a very strict legal hereditary system which eliminated the majority of possible candidates. Only legitimate sons of the Emperor were eligible for the succession: however it was not unusual that a ruler would favour an illegitimate son above those of legitimate birth, causing some confusion over the inheritance (see Chapter 10). In the event of there being no legitimate successor, the sons of the ruler's sisters were preferred to those of his brothers.

The nobility and the curacas also had principal wives and other, secondary wives. The highest nobility were given the privileged permission to marry their half sisters as their principal wives. The curacas, and the rest of the population did not normally marry their close kin, but could marry those removed to the fourth generation. The number of wives any man had was controlled, since these were considered to be luxury status symbols. Ideally, the nobles and curacas, followed a similar hereditary pattern as that described for the Emperor, although some of the curacas still retained a slight variation of the system based on local traditions of inheritance. Under the Inca system, hereditary posts were filled by the most able legitimate sons, or nearest relative in the female line. In the event of there being no adult legitimate son, the post could be filled by the brother of the deceased man, reverting to the latter's family when he died.

Each Inca ruler built his own palace in the centre of Cuzco from which he ruled. The royal palace had to be completely furnished with objects made especially for the new ruler; those of his predecessor were retained in his name by his panaca. Such a palace consisted of a number of simple well-built masonry structures, arranged around a series of courtyards, entered through a progression of closely guarded doorways. The Sapa Inca's own private quarters were located in the innermost part, and the whole complex was contained by an enclosure wall. The royal court, which consisted virtually of all the inner city of Cuzco, was continually filled with the nobles of royal blood and high ranking visitors from the provinces. Many of the most intelligent and informed elders of the empire were called upon to act as advisers to the Emperor in official, and unofficial, posts at his court. Others taught the sons of the nobles and foreign curacas in the schools called the *Yachahuasi*. In particular Pachacuti Inca, the great innovator, is said to have thrived in this atmosphere of learning and often visited the schools in order to discuss administrative and philosophical problems with both the amautas, and their pupils. Before the Emperor undertook any important project it was discussed with his advisors, the *Amauta-cuna*, and the Supreme Council. Pachacuti Inca (one account informs us) was democratic enough to submit his opinion in council to that of a majority! Such men, to whom the Emperor listened, were usually related to the royal family or held important social positions in their native lands; the ruling Sapa Inca did not believe it was easy to communicate with the low-born.

Every day the Emperor received numerous emissaries from the curacas and provincial governors. Cieza tells us the following about his day:

> From many of the lords of the country there came emissaries every day bringing gifts, and his court was filled with nobles, and his palaces with vessels and goblets of gold and silver and other great treasures. In the morning he took his repast, and from noon until late in the day he gave audience, accompanied by his guard, to whoever wished to talk with him. He then spent the rest of the day, until it was night, drinking, when he dined by the light of wood. . . . .

A person desiring to come into the Sapa Inca's presence, whatever his rank, took off his usuta sandals and put a token burden on his back to show his respect. Approaching the Emperor with lowered eyes the visitor made known his business, delivering his report or message. The Sapa Inca, who often sat behind a screen on a low stool, would then answer with few words, delivered quietly. Each Emperor seems to have increased his aura of superiority by additional details of behaviour and etiquette. In the case of Atahuallpa, his brother, the Inca Apu, was always present at interviews and the ruler would speak through him, rarely looking at or speaking directly to those of lower rank. Cieza describes an additional formality whereby the visitor stood with his back to the Emperor and bowed before speaking. These procedures applied only to those coming into the court from outside. Those who lived in the court or stayed for any length of time were usually of the nobility, or of high rank, and were therefore required to go through this procedure only on the first occasion, and not subsequently, when they entered the Emperor's presence. Only the highest nobility and officials in the land could be seated in the Emperor's presence, and these were also often present at interviews.

In each provincial capital as well as in Cuzco, the Sapa Inca had a raised platform called *usnu*, where he could sit on a carved, wooden stool, red in colour, from which he could preside over audiences and make judgements in his role as Emperor (25).

The Sapa Inca dressed in clothes of a type similar to those worn by his subjects, although certain of the designs were especially made for him; the finest materials, richly ornamented, were employed and sometimes distributed as gifts. The main symbol of his office, the *llauta*, consisted of a braid of many colours wound several times around his head. This supported the royal fringe, the *borla*, which stretched across the forehead between the temples and was made of red vicuña wool tassels hanging from little gold tubes. The heir to the throne wore a yellow fringe, smaller than his father's. The pompon, also supported by the braid, stood upward some 15 centimetres (6 in.) from the forehead on a stick and sported three feathers from the rare *corequenque* bird. The Sapa Inca's hair style was short and he wore the largest gold earplugs the lobes could be stretched to receive.

The Sapa Inca's personal needs were carefully attended to by his concubine wives. They prepared his food for him and served it in dishes of gold, silver and pottery, placing these before him on on rush matting. The Sapa Inca sat on his stool and ate with his fingers from plates held by the women. Normally he ate alone and only his legitimate sons were supposed to be privileged enough to eat with him on occasion. Juan Ruiz de Arce describes the attentions he saw Atahuallpa's women paid him:

If he hawked or spat a woman held out her hand and he spat into it. And any hairs that fell from his head on to his clothes were picked up by the women and eaten. The reason for these customs is known: the spitting was out of majesty; the hairs because he was afraid of being bewitched.

This sort of attention is not remarked on in the case of any of the other rulers, and the inference is that Atahuallpa was slightly

25 *The Sapa Inca seated on his usnu throne*
26 *The Sapa Inca travelling in a litter with his Coya*

paranoid, due to his position as an usurper. For all these attentions, however, the Emperor, the Divine Son of the Sun, like his subjects, slept on the ground, the impact of which was softened by a cotton quilted cloth and a warm covering of woollen blankets.

When the Emperor travelled, to visit the provinces or to accompany his army, or even to visit his pleasure resorts, his journey was well organized, and he was carried in a litter. The litter consisted of a boxed-in, carved passenger seat set between two long poles of the finest wood, adorned with gold and silver (*26*). These litters were extremely luxurious, built to seat either one person or two people facing each other, seated among cushions. Some had coats of arms, ornamented in gold, silver and precious stones: the insignia consisting of the Sun, the Moon, or serpents intertwined around a staff. Over the litter there rose two arches ornamented with gold and set with precious stones, which supported a feathered canopy, or from which long curtains were hung in order to cover in the occupant. The Emperor usually travelled with his curtains drawn, and, since they had holes for air (also providing a view of the road), they were raised only for exit and entry. Runners went ahead to announce his coming and if the Sapa Inca raised the curtain, en route, those who came out to line the royal road and watch him pass would cry out in great excitement: 'Most great and mighty Lord, Son of the Sun, thou alone art our Lord, may the entire world hearken unto you.'

The litters were borne on the shoulders of men from the two provinces of the Rucunas. These men were carefully selected and trained for this office from the age of 20, and were chosen for their sturdiness and the smooth gait they maintained in difficult terrain. Up to 20 bearers carried the Inca so that if one of them stumbled, it was hardly noticed. (Stumbling was however severely punished.) Replacements travelled in the Inca's train.

Pachacuti Inca, as Emperor, was the first Inca ruler to make a visitation to the territory he ruled. For the occasion he ordered lodgings to be built along the main roads, spaced out to provide an easy day's journey—about 20 kilometres (12 miles)—between each. He travelled in great pomp, with his Coya and other wives in hammock litters, carrying many loads of jewels and other riches in his royal train. His guard and archers surrounded him on foot; behind the train came an equal number of lancers and their captains; and in front of the entourage, the road cleaners weeded out every blade of grass and removed obstacles from the road surface. Taking with him, also, advisers and many members of the court, each Emperor sought to travel in more pomp than his father had done before him and in addition to improve upon and widen the roads. Huayna Capac ordered 50,000 troops to accompany him on one visit through the kingdom. Supplies for the Emperor and his train were provided from the storehouses along the route and baggage was carried by the people of one town to the next, where new bearers took over.

While the ruler was absent from Cuzco he entrusted the administration to an uncle, brother, or other close relative. Similarly when he was not able to accompany the army to further his conquests, he chose a close relative to lead it as Commander-in-Chief. This was a dangerous position for anyone to maintain, except perhaps for the heir, since any incompetence displayed (or even too much success) could lead to the Inca Emperor's anger, probably resulting in the offender's prompt execution, as in the case of Capac Yupanqui (p. 27).

Most of the Inca rulers seem to have lived into ripe old age. When an Emperor died it naturally caused great consternation and his family were responsible for organizing the details of elaborate ceremonial. Upon his death it was said that the Inca's father, the Sun, had recalled him. There followed a period of prolonged weeping and sacrifices during which muffled drums were played. The amautas (elders) discussed his history and sent for the quipucamayocs to compose works to be sung universally in his honour. The mourning period lasted a year and was organized into three main stages. We are told that at Huayna Capac's death the lamentations and shrieks 'rose to the skies causing the birds to fall to the ground'.

After death the entrails were removed, placed in a special receptacle and then buried at Tampu (near Ollantaytambo). Then the Inca's body was preserved by some means, which probably included the use of herbs for drying. The chroniclers reported that the bodies of the dead rulers achieved a remarkably life-like appearance with the use of some bitumen substance after the bodies had dried out in the cold dry air of the sierra mountains. The eyes of the mummy were carefully replaced with permanent life-like replicas made of inlaid shells.

Garcilaso remembers touching one of the Inca Huayna Capac's fingers 'which seemed like that of a wooden statue, it was so hard and stiff'. After a body had been embalmed it was placed before the figure of the Sun in the temple of Cuzco and many sacrifices were offered to it.

Although some of his favourite women and most useful servants were supposed voluntarily to accompany the dead Inca ruler into the other world in order to serve him there, they were not always as willing as the records might lead one to believe; they were made drunk during the festivities and were then strangled. The highest figure recorded for such an event was 5,000 people, killed to accompany the Inca Huayna Capac. However, it seems likely that this figure was highly inflated and it is even doubtful whether this custom was an Inca one.

During the year following the Inca ruler's death the special songs and narratives composed were sung throughout the empire by professional mourners of both sexes, and pilgrimages were organized by the new Sapa Inca to honour his father. Banners were made of some of the Inca's clothes and were carried to places he had frequented during his life. Many women, all over the empire, cut off their hair, binding their heads with hempen ropes. At the end of the year a final ceremony called *cullu huacani* was held when everyone stopped the pain by washing themselves with black soap (sooty ashes).

The bodies of the deceased Inca rulers were kept in the palace

27 *Mummies of the dead rulers were brought out for important occasions*

each had inhabited during his lifetime. Here, among all their treasures and belongings, they were carefully attended, waited on as in life by their descendants, who also brought the bodies out for public ceremonials (27). On such occasions the mummies were carried in their litters dressed and adorned in their best finery, covered with gold and seated on the duho stools. In death, an Inca became an idol which was worshipped and consulted as an oracle. His power therefore survived through his kin, who were responsible for interpreting his responses when he was required to give any answers!

The Coyas were also buried with pomp and considerable treasure, and in some cases they too were maintained as mummies, as if in life. Some scholars consider that the quantity of waste incurred in supporting the increasing number of dead Incas in such state, and the continued practice of making sacrifices to them, was a factor in the political confrontation between the Inca Huascar and the royal family in 1528 (see Chapter 10).

THE COYA

The Coya did not lack for her share of importance as the first lady of the empire. As the Emperor's consort and full sister, she was held in very high esteem and revered for her womanly virtues. The qualities most admired in her were discretion, understanding and grave comportment, which might have proved rather limiting! However, in reality each of the Coyas seems to have had very different characteristics and some were evidently quite eccentric: Poma even depicts one Coya, the fifth queen called Chinbo Mama, lying on the ground having an epileptic fit. He shows the eleventh Coya, Raya Ocllo (wife of Huayna Capac), at her toilet (9).

As Empress, the Coya was supposed to play a role complimentary to that of the Emperor, cultivating interests in religion, prayer, entertainments and horticulture—while the ruler concerned himself with administration, wars, and other more masculine pursuits. In the chronicles, the Coya is portrayed in a rather idealized way, often as being entirely complimentary to the Sapa Inca—so that some of his actions are attributed to her. This is particularly confusing when the Emperor's peacetime legislation is described as activated by the Coya (Murua's chronicle) in her role of his representative in Cuzco, while he was engaged in new conquests. Certainly in religious and ceremonial ritual she played an active part, complimentary to that of the Sapa Inca. The cult of the Moon was dedicated to her in shrines throughout the empire, placed near and attendant upon those of the Sun. In some instances a temple was also dedicated to her. Topa Inca ordered a temple to be built in honour of his sister wife, Mama Ocllo, and Huayna Capac constructed an imposing shrine to house this Coya's mummy.

Among her active duties in public ceremonial life the Coya played a key role at agricultural festivals in the rituals. In connection with this role, her garden was highly praised for its varied species of plants, flowers, wild and tame animals. Her place was evidently well defined in the Inca concept of the ideal woman: chaste patroness of fertility, spiritual, yet earthy.

The Coya had her own special palace or lodgings in Cuzco, with her coat-of-arms, the Rainbow, painted over the entrance. She lived with the royal maidens, the ñusta, who were her ladies in waiting. The Coya ate alone and was served by the ñusta and servants. She bathed twice a day and gave her dresses away to the ñusta. She was often entertained by her court jesters, and jugglers (who juggled with their feet). When she went out she walked beneath a canopy of feathers of many colours and silver bells. She was accompanied by two ñusta, one at each arm, and was preceded by servants who advanced in pairs, putting cloths on the ground for her to step on.

THE HEIR

The heir to the Emperor was carefully trained and prepared for his future role by the amautas, from whom he received schooling in deciphering the quipus, learning history and literature from them, and studying such subjects as elementary geometry, basic mathematical problems, engineering and administration. His curriculum also included preparation for battle, military strategy, and physical training. As an athlete he was expected to outshine the sons of the nobility and curaca at the games in the knighting ceremony. On passing these puberty tests he was expected to take an active part in military conquests.

In the choice of a suitable heir the Incas had to consider not only a legitimate son, but one who was intelligent and had administrative capabilities; equally important, someone who would continue to expand the empire and the prestige of the Incas. Pachacuti Inca reversed his choice of heir from Amaru Topa Inca to Topa Inca Yupanqui, because he considered that the former would not satisfy the people's need for military conquests—he was too peace-loving.

As soon as the prince was knighted, he could take secondary wives (concubines) without any special ceremony. His father might give him his first wife as a gift, in which case it was likely that she would be chosen for her looks from among the daughters of the newly conquered curacas. Later, he was formally married to his principal wife, his sister, but only on assuming the Incaship.

The heir prepared himself for his coronation by withdrawing into seclusion, where he fasted, eating only maize, and abstaining from women. The coronation ceremony began with the heir nominated by the Emperor being presented to the royal family and the Inca nobility for their approval, and then being presented to the Sun. In the ceremony held in the Temple of the Sun, Coricancha, the new Sapa Inca, took possession of his office by placing the borla on his forehead, and receiving the other insignia of office: the *Sunturpaucar* (the pompon and its three feathers of the sacred Corenquenque bird), the *champi* (warclub), and a banner on which were painted the rainbow and two snakes. After the ceremony in the Sun Temple there were great feasts and sacrifices were made. The new Inca ruler sat upon the throne, usnu, in the great square, where every noble and curaca able to reach Cuzco had assembled. Each in turn did him homage and presented him with a white feather, each in turn, signifying their allegiance.

However, the coronation of each of the Inca rulers in the empire period occured in different circumstances. Pachacuti Inca Yupanqui, who assumed the leadership in order to save Cuzco from the Chanca attack, and evidently against his father's wishes, had himself crowned while his father lived in retirement. Pachacuti was extremely careful to avoid a divided political scene over the succession when he died. He called together the royal family in Cuzco and named Topa Inca Yupanqui as his heir. Sarmiento describes what must have been an idealized pattern for the upbringing of the heir, as recorded in the Inca traditions, although not necessarily followed in the same sequence. After years of careful education and instruction from his tutors 'in the House of the Sun', Topa Inca was presented to the royal family as the heir and his investiture is described as follows:

He [Pachacuti Inca] named his son Tupac Inca, and ordered him to come forth from the house. . . . He was now shown to the people, and the Inca presently ordered a fringe of gold to be placed in the hand of the image of the Sun, with the head-dress called *pillaca-llauta*. After Tupac Inca had made his obeisance to his father, the Inca and the rest rose and went before the image of the Sun where they made their sacrifices and offered *capa cocha* to that deity. Then they offered the new Inca Tupac Yupanqui, beseeching the Sun to protect and foster him, and to make him so that all should hold and judge him to be a child of the Sun and father of his people. This done the oldest and principal *orejones* [Incas] took Tupac Inca to the Sun, and the priests took the fringe from the hands of the image, which they call *mascapay-cha*, and placed it over the head of Tupac Inca Yupanqui until it rested on his forehead. He was declared Inca Ccapac and seated in front of the Sun on a seat of gold, called *duho*, garnished with emeralds and other precious stones. Seated there, they clothed him in the *capac hongo* [or *uncu* 'tunic'], placed the *suntur paucar* in his hand, gave him the insignia of Inca, and the priests raised him on their shoulders. When these ceremonies were completed, Pachacuit Inca Yupanqui ordered that his son Tupac Inca should remain shut up in the House of the Sun, performing the fasts which it is customary to go through before receiving the order of chivalry [*Huarachico*].

After being knighted in the Huarachico ceremony (p. 79) Pachacuti Inca presented Topa Inca with his sister, Mama Ocllo. Later, when Pachacuti died, the Incas again invested Topa Inca with the fringe and gave him the other insignia of sovereignty, then they escorted him with his guard to the great square, where he was seated in majesty on the usnu throne. Only then, according to Sarmiento, did Topa Inca announce the death of his father. Other accounts, concerning the coronations of Huayna Capac and Huascar Inca, plainly describe the coronation ceremony taking place after the death and an initial mourning period for the deceased ruler. This practice was, however, not ideal since inaction could leave loopholes for intrigue, as happened in the case of the Inca Huayna Capac, whose investiture was not completed in time: his brothers vied with one another for the throne while he was protected during his fast in Quispicancha palace outside Cuzco. He in turn died unexpectedly and left the succession in confusion (see Chapter 10).

4

Family life and ritual

28 Quirau, cradle

BIRTH AND CHILD-REARING

When a woman was pregnant she continued to fulfil all her home tasks, although she did no agricultural work. Children were considered an economic asset and any attempt at abortion was severely punished by the execution of the culprit and anyone who aided her. Known methods of abortion included beatings, fetal massages and special drugs.

Before the child was born the mother was supposed to confess and pray for an easy delivery, while the husband was meant to fast during the delivery. Although midwives as such were unknown, mothers of twins were considered to have special powers and were sometimes present to help with the birth. Many women delivered without assistance and were able to take themselves and the baby to the nearest water source to wash. The mother then resumed normal household tasks, usually immediately. If she bore twins, however, or the baby had some defect, the family considered it a bad omen and fasted, performing certain rituals to counter-act this. On the fourth day after birth the baby was put in a *quirau* (cradle) (*28*), to which it was tied, and its relatives were invited around to see it and drink chicha. A commoner carried her child in a cradle on her back, which was supported with a shawl tied over the chest when she went out and wished to take the child with her.

Garcilaso, who was himself brought up by his Palla mother in the Inca tradition, gives an interesting account of the upbringing of children under Inca regime:

They brought up their children in a strange way, both Incas and common folk, rich and poor, without distinction, with the least possible pampering. As soon as the baby was born it was washed in water and wrapped in shawls. Every morning when it was wrapped up it was washed in cold water, and often exposed to the night air and dew. When the mother wanted to pamper her child, she would take the water into her mouth and then wash it all over, except the head, and especially the crown, which was never washed. It was said that this accustomed the babies to cold and hardship, and also that it strengthened their limbs. Their arms were kept inside the swaddling clothes for more than three months, because it was thought that if they were loosened earlier, they would grow weak in the arm. They were kept lying in their cradles, which were sort of rough benches on four legs with one leg shorter than the others so that they could be rocked. The bed on which the baby reclined was a coarse net which was only a little less hard than the bare boards: the same net was used to hitch the baby to the sides of the cradle and tie it up so that it could not fall out.

The mothers never took the babies into their arms or on their laps either when giving suck or at any other time. They said it made them crybabies, and encouraged them to want to be nursed and not to stay in the cradle. The mother bent over the baby and gave it her breast. This was done thrice a day, in the morning, at midday, and in the evening. Except at these times no milk was given, even if they cried. Otherwise it was thought they would get used to sucking all day long and develop dirty habits with vomiting and diarrhea, and grow up to be greedy and gluttonous men. . . . The mother reared the child herself, and never gave it out to nurse, even if she were a great lady, unless she were ill. During this time they abstained from sexual intercourse, considering that it spoiled the milk and caused the baby to pine and grow weak.

The child was breast-fed as long as the mother had milk. When the child was old enough to be moved from the cradle, Garcilaso says, a hole was made in the ground for it to jump about and play in. The hole came up to the child's armpits and was lined with a few rags and contained some toys for its amusement. This device may have been used in special circumstances as a sort of play pen, perhaps in the Incas' gardens, but Garcilaso does not elaborate on the whereabouts of this pit. He also describes how, when the child was old enough to crawl about, 'it approached its mother from one side or the other to be suckled, which it did kneeling on the ground', presumably while the mother sat on the ground herself.

29 Older children help their parents: tending animals collecting firewood and killing birds

The child was named later at a special ceremony called *Rutuchico* meaning the 'cutting of the hair'. This was performed when the child was weaned, at one to two years old. All the relations attended this ceremony and sometimes friends of the family. After a feast the eldest, or most important, male relative started off the haircutting by removing a lock of the child's hair. Each person who cut a lock offered the child a gift. The hair and nails were thus cut and carefully preserved.

When this ceremony was performed on the Emperor's son, each noble, in order of importance, cut off a lock of the prince's hair and offered him rich gifts of fine clothes and jewellery of gold and silver, revering him as a grandson of the Sun.

The names given to children at the Rutuchico were used only until they reached maturity. During this period most children followed their parents about and learnt by copying them and helping them in their daily tasks. Unproductive play was not encouraged, and from childhood everyone learned all the crafts required for their everyday needs, such as making simple clothes, shoes and utensils, cooking and agriculture. Male children helped their parents in looking after their animals, chasing birds and pests from their fields (29). Girls helped their mothers with the new babies and there were always plenty of simple household tasks requiring attention, such as sewing, cooking, washing and cleaning.

EDUCATION

There was no formal education available for most of the sons of the commoners, except for the trades that they learnt from their parents. The following quote from an Inca ruler's sayings sums up the attitude of the nobility:

> It is not right that the children of plebians should be taught knowledge that is only suitable for nobles, lest the lower classes rise up and grow arrogant and bring down the republic: it is enough that they learn the trades of their fathers, for governing is no matter for them, and it is discreditable to power and to the state that these should be entrusted to the common people.

Some of the girls, daughters of commoners, might however be selected for education in the provincial *Acllahuasi*, the House of the Virgins. These were convents in which the Chosen Women— *Mamacunas* (Consecrated Women) and *Acllas* (Virgins) lived (see Chapter 9). In each province an agent, the *Apupanaca*, was appointed by the Emperor to select the girls and be responsible for organizing their keep in the Acllahuasi. He travelled to all the villages choosing the 'prettiest, of best appearance and disposition' from amongst girls aged nine to ten years old. These girls lived in the provincial capitals under the care of the Mamacunas—nuns dedicated to teaching—who prepared them for their future. The Mamacunas taught the girls religion and womanly chores: to dye, spin, and weave wool and cotton to a high standard; to cook food and to make fine chicha, especially chicha prepared for sacrificial rites. When the girls reached the age of 13–14 they were taken to Cuzco by the Apupanaca for the Inti Raymi, Festival of the Sun.

In Cuzco the Acllas were presented to the Emperor who was then responsible for deciding on their future. The most beautiful girls became the servants or concubine wives of the Inca himself, or were given by him to those he wished to honour or reward for their services, usually Incas and curacas. Others were kept for special sacrifices, to serve in the shrines or to live in the convents where they instructed future generations of Acllas.

All the sons of Incas and curacas were obliged to attend the *Yachahuasi* (House of Teaching) in the capital, Cuzco. In the case of the latter, the privilege of attendance was double-edged. On the one hand they had the advantage of living in the Inca court all the year round and of receiving an education in the Inca culture. This, however, also served as indoctrination, and created in them favourable attitudes to Inca policies for the time when they inherited posts from their fathers. Meanwhile they were useful hostages for the Sapa Inca to ensure the loyalty of their provinces and the curacas.

Of life in the schools Garcilaso writes:

> As they had no book-learning, the teaching was done by practice, daily use, and experience, and in this way they learned the rites, precepts, and ceremonies of their false religion and came to understand the reason and basis of their laws and privileges, the number of them, and their true interpretation. They attained the knowledge of how to govern and became more civilized and better skilled in the art of war. They learnt about the times and seasons of the year and could record and read history from the knots. They learned to speak with elegance and taste, and to bring up their children and to govern their houses. They were taught poetry, music, philosophy, and astrology, or such little as was known of these sciences. The masters were called amautas—'Philosophers' or 'Wise men'—and were held in high esteem. [In fact there was no abstract philosophy, only direct observation of reality—*Author*]

Rowe says the course of study took four years, each of which was devoted to a different subject: Quechua in the first year, Religion in the second, Quipus in the third, and Inca History in the fourth. Discipline was kept by beatings of up to ten blows on the soles of the feet—though teachers were restricted to meting out one beating a day!

PUBERTY

Puberty rites were held for girls and boys, called *Quicochico* and *Huarachico* respectively.

There was no formal collective ceremony for the girls, with the possible exception of the participation of the daughters of the nobility on the occasion of the boy's Huarachico (p. 80). Quicochico, a family affair, was celebrated when a girl had her first menstruation. In preparation she remained at home fasting for three days, while her mother wove her a new outfit. She emerged on the fourth, was washed, her hair was braided, and she was dressed in the fine new clothes and sandals of white wool. Meanwhile her relatives had gathered for a two-day feast to celebrate the occasion, at which it was her duty to serve them. Afterwards, everyone gave her gifts and she received a permanent name from her most important male relative, who gave her good advice and told her to obey and serve her parents to the best of her ability.

Women's names suggested qualities admired and considered

suitable for a female to have, so that a girl might be named after an object or an abstract quality—such as Ocllo (Pure) or Cori (Gold). An unusual name was given one of the Coyas who was called Mama Runto (Runto meaning Egg) because she had a lighter complexion than most Andean women, and the comparison was considered an elegant figure of speech. Boys were given titles and names evocative of qualities or characteristics of animals: Yupanqui (Honoured), Amaru (Dragon), Poma (Puma), Cusi (Happy), Titu (Liberal).

The boys took part in the puberty ceremony called Huarachico when they were about 14, give or take a year. This was one of the most traditional of the Inca rituals, held each year for the sons of noblemen in Cuzco. Although at its most ceremonious and important in Cuzco, puberty rites were also held at the same time in the provincial capitals under the direction of Inca governors, for the sons of local nobles. Similarly, a simpler celebration also marked the puberty of the commoners, at which the boys were given their first breechcloths made for them by their mothers.

Accounts of this festival are interwoven with the great feast of Capac Raymi, which was held during the same month (our December) when the provinces sent their tributes to the Inca Emperor in Cuzco. Two full accounts, that of Garcilaso and that of Cobo vary greatly so that it is almost impossible to integrate them. Briefly, Cobo's account describes elaborate ceremonies, sacrifices, rituals and dancing, while sports, athletics and military games play a very secondary role. On the other hand Garcilaso's account is detailed in its description of endurance tests: a long-distance race from Huanacauri to Cuzco, a mock battle in the fortress above the town, wrestling, jumping, throwing, and marksmanship contests. According to Garcilaso the boys were tested as sentinels, for their resistance to pain, and for courage; furthermore, they had to show they could make their own weapons and usuta sandals in an emergency. Garcilaso's account may, however, be coloured by his own experience of the Huarachico as a mestizo (half-breed), since the Spaniards attempted to re-orientate the indian ceremonies away from their underlying religious implications. In this case, it is probable that Cobo's account is the more reliable.

The main Huarachico rites coincided, as we have seen, with the celebrated festival of Capac Raymi, but preparations for Huarachico were begun well in advance. Special outfits were woven by the women for their sons: narrow shirts made from fine vicuña wool, and narrow white mantles which fastened at the neck by a cord from which hung a red tassel. Meanwhile the candidates went to the shrine of Huanacauri, about six-and-a-half kilometres (four miles) from Cuzco, where they made sacrifices to the idol, asking permission to enter the knighthood. The priests gave each boy a sling and drew a line on his face with the blood of the llama that had been sacrificed. The boys then collected ichu grass for their parents to sit on. Upon returning to Cuzco, everyone prepared for the coming festivities by making vast quantities of chicha.

On the first day of the month the nobles presented their sons to the Sun, their ancestor, in the Temple of the Sun. The boys were dressed in their special home-made outfits and so were their kinfolk. Next, they all went to Huanacauri, taking with them a sacred white llama. The following morning more sacrifices and rituals were performed at the Huanacauri shrine before the return to Cuzco. During the return a curious ritual was enacted: the parents whipped the boys' legs with slings. Upon arrival in Cuzco they made sacrifices to idols and the mummies of ancestors in the central square.

After a few days' rest, during which the boys probably fasted, the families reassembled in the central square, this time in the presence of the Sapa Inca, for more celebration and ritual, which would eventually lead to the awarding of the knighthoods. The boys—and the girls—who were to serve in the festivities, were given outfits from the storehouses of the Sun by the high priest. The boys clothing consisted of striped red and white shirts and a white mantle which had a blue cord and red tassle; they also wore special usuta sandals, made of ichu grass for the occasion by their male kin. At this point everyone moved towards Huanacauri, for the hill of Anahuarque, where after more sacrifices the Incas danced their special Taqui dance. This was followed by the ritual of a foot race. The boys, watched and cheered on by their relatives, raced for a distance of about 1,000 metres, (1,100 yds) down a dangerous slope. They were met at the finishing post at the bottom of the slope by the girls, who waited upon them with tumblers of chicha.

Next, after returning again to Cuzco, they set out for the hills of Sabaraura and Yavira, where further sacrifices and dances were performed. Here the boys were given their insignia of maturity, the breechcloth and gold ear-plugs, by the Sapa Inca. After again dancing the Taqui, everyone returned to Cuzco, repeating the ritual of whipping the boys' legs, to do homage to the gods. After these numerous ceremonies, the new knights went to bathe in a fountain called *Calipuquio*, behind the fortress of Cuzco, where they placed the clothes which they had worn for the ceremonies and put on other clothing called *nanaclla*, which was coloured black and yellow. Finally, on returning to the central square of Cuzco, the Huacapata, they were given presents by their families, including weapons from their godfathers, and lectured on how they should comport themselves as adults and were told to be brave and loyal to the Emperor and revere the gods.

MARRIAGE

After the puberty rites, sons and daughters continued to live at home and serve their parents (*29*) until they married and set up a house of their own. Although the Sapa Inca, the Inca nobility and curacas had many or several wives, a principal wife and and secondary wives (concubines), few of the commoners were able to possess more than one wife.

The principal wife was not necessarily the first woman taken, but she was the only one taken in a proper marriage ceremony conducted with official supervision and a wedding at home. Other wives, however, could only be obtained as rewards, distributed either by the Emperor or by important administrators. Although prior to the empire period incest was forbidden, the custom was altered for the nobility and most Inca men found a principal wife from among their female relatives. Only marriages with all direct ancestors and direct descendants were prohibited to everyone. The Sapa Inca was the only person permitted to marry his full sister, but those of royal blood married within the fourth degree, so that there were many royal children of legitimate blood. The men of the highest aristocracy were given the privilege of marrying their half-sisters, but not those born of the same mother. Provincial commoners, however, could be given the death penalty if they married within the fourth degree, although they were obliged to marry within their ayllu (local kinship group). Typical marriages within these local groups might consist of an exchange of sisters between two men. Girls usually married between 16 and 20, while young men married a little older, usually by 25.

The heir to the throne married his sister only on completion of the formalities regarding his succession. The description of such a marriage is recorded by Pachacuti Yamqui who says that Huayna Capac departed from his grandfather's (Pachacuti) house, with his council and the Apocuraca and high state officials of Collasuyu; his sister Mama Cusirimay left her father's (Topa Yupanqui) palace and accompanied by all the auquiconas and the great Apocuracas of Chinaysuyu, Cuntisuyu and Antisuyu. Each procession progressed towards the Temple of the Sun while 50,000 warriors guarded the city. Mama Cusirimay was carried on her father's litter, Huayna Capac on his grandfather's and each entered the temple through a different door. The High Priest joined them in wedlock and then there followed the customary feasting and dancing.

Other young couples throughout the empire first had to obtain their 'licence' to marry at a brief betrothal ceremony, perhaps nearer to our registry office marriages. These ceremonies were conducted once a year and were inaugurated in Cuzco, when the Sapa Inca ordered all the marriageable girls and young men of his lineage, to gather together in the main plaza. To bind a couple legally the Sapa Inca took each by the hand, united them and delivered them to their parents. On the following day the appointed officials married the sons and daughters of other residents in the city, keeping separate the divisions of Hanan and Hurin Cuzco. Elsewhere, throughout the empire this ceremony was performed by the local curacas, Hunu Curaca, with an Inca administrator present. Weddings were then solemnized in the presence of the nearest relatives.

The bridegroom, accompanied by his parents, then visited his bride's family to fetch her. On arrival he acknowledged her by putting a sandal on her right foot—if she was a virgin the sandal was of white wool, if not, it was made of ichu grass—and took her hand. Next the relatives of both groups took her to the bridegroom's house. Arriving there, the girl gave her new husband a fine woollen shirt, a *lautto*, and a flat metal ornament, which he put on. The couple's parents then remained until nightfall lecturing them on their marital duties: the bride's parents told her how she was to serve her husband, while his parents lectured him on how he should treat his wife. Celebrations, including feasting and drinking, were held in the community, the extent of which varied with the economic status of the families.

The newly married couple started their life in a house specially built for them and household requirements were given as gifts by the relatives who brought one gift each. In the case of the nobility, the house was built by the mit'a—a public works force of indians from the provinces. Commoners also received gifts from relatives, but had their house built for them by the local community in the quarter to which their parents belonged. One of the main reasons for the restriction of marriages to within local groups was that intermarriage, within a group of 10 to 100 families, simplified the organization of population.

The family marriage formalities, after the usual official betrothal, varied according to local traditions in each area of the empire. For instance, in the Collao the bridegroom took a small bag of coca leaves to offer his mother-in-law and on its acceptance the marriage was completed. In other places the bridegroom offered to work four or five days for his bride's parents, taking them firewood and ichu grass. Trial marriages, during which a couple lived under the same roof, were also common in some areas. While elopement without the father's consent was not encouraged, the law permitted it as long as both parties were of the same village and the desire to marry was mutual (p.86).

There were important differences between the position of the legitimate wife and the secondary wives or concubines. The latter had to obey the principal wife, who was also served by them. While the principal wife was secure in her married status until her death, the concubines could be got rid of quite easily.

The Sapa Inca usually took his concubines from girls of royal blood. Virgins of the Sun, of royal blood educated in Cuzco, could become concubines or wives of the Incas or of the Inca himself, before they were consecrated, but not the wives (principal or otherwise) of ordinary people who were not descended from the Sun. Illegitimate daughters were considered to have lost this imaginary divinity and it was therefore considered all right to give them in marriage to an important curaca.

The Sapa Inca also gave away women—for wives or concubines —from among the Acllas, brought to Cuzco once a year. When the tribute had been gathered from all over the empire, the Emperor divided the Acllas, who had been brought to Cuzco by the provincial Apupanaca, into their three categories (p.77). Those that were destined to be wives and concubines were then divided between the nobility, Incas and curacas. The girl's future status depended on whether the man to whom she would be given had already married a principal wife. If he had, she would be a secondary wife and was sent to him without any further ceremony, but if she was given to an unmarried man, she might be given the status of the principal wife and the formal marriage ceremony would be celebrated, even if he was a widower.

It was strictly prohibited for a man to marry one of his secondary wives after the death of his principal wife. Instead, he appointed one of the secondary wives as temporary head of the household until he married another principal wife. This law was to prevent jealousies and ambitious competition between secondary wives plotting to replace the legal wife. It was also forbidden to take close kin as secondary wives.

One of the duties of a secondary wife in a large household of an important man, was to act as a nanny to a legitimate son. In this case, she was 'given' to the son and was responsible for washing and looking after the boy until he reached puberty, when her role changed and she became his sleeping partner, initiating him into the pleasures of sex. When eventually the boy married, the woman remained with him. A son also inherited any of his father's secondary wives who had not borne him children, when the father died.

A somewhat similar practice existed in the case of orphans, when they were given to a childless widow. A male child would be brought up by a widow and educated in sex once he had passed the puberty rites. The young man remained with her until he married; then it was his duty to support her as a secondary wife until he paid back the debt he owed her. Unless she was inherited by her husband's brother, it was difficult for a widow to remarry.

Although it was rare for a commoner to be given a second wife, these were sometimes acquired with army service, where the man might be allowed to keep a woman he had captured, but, presumably, only if she had no living legal husband.

ADULT MALE LIFE

Once married, a man was considered fully adult and he started to fulfil a more responsible role in the organization of the empire. If he was an Inca, or the son of a curaca, he might be given an official post in some branch of administration or he might serve in the army. Otherwise, he could live at court or, if his family owned lands, he could live off the yield from these. He started his married life with one great advantage, as a member of the élite he did not have to pay tribute.

A commoner, once married was automatically counted in the census as a tribute payer. This was not only due to the fact that he was now considered fully adult, but that with marriage he became a householder and received a small area of community land to cultivate for his family needs. He was given a full year to settle into his new life and start a family before demands began to be made of him, and then there were numerous ways in which these demands could be made. He had to help with the agricultural work on the lands of the Sun and the Inca Emperor (p. 145), and on those of his local curaca. He might also have to participate in any community projects or work that had to be carried out locally, and he was liable to about five years' total service (sometime between the age of 25 and 50) in one of the three main tribute-supported mit'a services of the empire: the army, the public works force, or the mines. The only way a commoner could hope to better his lot was to outshine his fellows in the army; through outstanding service he might obtain the recognition of his superiors and win some rewards or even advancement in his status. In this case, rewards might consist of the right to wear certain insignia or possess some luxurious goods in his home. An advancement in status is less clear: he could become a local leader of ten or even 50 tribute-payers, or he might, in unusual circumstances, receive another woman, or a gift of land with tribute exemption. The latter, however, was probably reserved for the Incas and curacas, who were in any case normally exempt from tribute payments.

There were sometimes certain additional demands made by the government on the householder. Male children under ten years old could be demanded for sacrifice. Such sacrifices were relatively rare and the demands were only made of a father of several children. A father might also have to give up a daughter if the Apupanaca chose her for an Aclla. The man was not allowed to refuse under any circumstances, unless he could prove she had already been defiled—and this involved proving a criminal offence.

In the home, the men were responsible for making footwear for their families, a craft which some chroniclers describe as one of the requirements made of those entering the knighthood. The Incas and curacas had servants to make their sandals, but they also sometimes deigned to make their own footwear or weapons. Most of the chroniclers make some reference to tribes in Ecuador where the women worked in the fields and men in the house, but this was not an Inca custom; such unusual local customs could reflect the fact that few males survived the Inca conquest in some areas, or the combination of the civil war, Spanish conquest and pestilences brought by the Europeans.

The Andeans were not too concerned with the virginity of their women before marriage—but more for their economic qualities as hard-working, willing and affectionate companions, which was tested in a trial period of some months before obtaining licence to marry. Not all marriages were successful, but a man was held responsible for the well-being of his wife. If she sickened the priest usually ordered him to fast, and if she died it could prove difficult for a man to marry again since he might be suspected of causing her death. If a man threw out his legitimate wife he was under an obligation to take her back; if he then tried again to be rid of her, he received a public punishment.

A saying attributed to Pachacuti Inca outlines the Inca attitude to adultery: 'Adulterers who destroy the reputation and rank of others and take away their peace and happiness should

30 Punishments (according to Poma): *a sorcerer's family is clubbed to death for taking life; hanging by the hair was the punishment for seducing an Aclla; stoning was the punishment meted out for adultery*

be considered thieves, and therefore be condemned to death without any reprieve.' How the law was enforced depended on who the culprits were. Adultery committed between a commoner and a woman of consequence, was very serious—both were executed (*30*). Adultery committed between two persons of different provinces was punished by torture, while that committed between two persons of the same locality was considered less serious; even so, there was a law which stated that a husband who killed his wife for adultery was set free without punishment. To ensure that this law was not taken advantage of another clause was added: if he killed her in a rage, to get rid of her, he was given the death penalty.

Other laws, which concerned the individual, were similar to our laws today, but some of the punishments were harsher: rape was punished with a heavy stone being dropped on the man's shoulders for a first offence, and the death penalty on the second. Robbers by habit were banished to the Andes hotlands, where they worked on coca plantations. Homicide was punished by execution if the survivor had begun the quarrel that led to the homicide. If the quarrel had been started by the deceased, the defendant was freed and any punishment was at discretion of the judge. Wounding or causing bodily harm to another was punished arbitrarily —but he who lamed another in a quarrel, so that he couldn't work, was obliged to support him from his own land and also to suffer some punishment. If he had no land the man was fed from the Inca's stores and the culprit was more severely punished. Destruction of government property, for example, burning a bridge, a storehouse, or other structure, was a serious offence punished with the death penalty. Disobedience and lying were both punished and continuing offenders received the death penalty; the third time for disobedience and the second time for perjury. Similarly, a show of disrespect to the Emperor or his government merited imprisonment. Bribery was a serious offence by which an official could lose his office and, if the offence was very serious, even receive the death penalty.

There were also laws concerning the traveller. Since subjects were not allowed to move provinces, they had to have permission to travel from their curaca, and a mitima (colonist) who left his new home was tortured, receiving the death penalty for a second offence. Changing dress and appearance emblems was considered one of the more serious of crimes; this was punished vigorously by everyone concerned, the government and the province. But the Incas really showed their puritanical streak in the way sodomy and 'vices' were punished. Such crimes were the most harshly dealt with. Not only the couples concerned but their families also were executed and their houses burnt as if to disinfect the area from such perverted behaviour! Other crimes which involved punishing the whole family were treason and murder by sorcery (30).

ADULT FEMALE LIFE

Women of all ages and status were theoretically free from tribute-paying. They were expected to serve their husbands to the best of their ability in whatever tasks there were to be done (which varied of course according to his rank). He in turn was supposed to look after her interests and see that she was well looked after and able to carry out his demands.

A commoner's wife shared in her husband's duties as a taxpayer; she and the children aided him in the community agricultural work and served him at home. Each family was expected to make one woven garment a year for the government, with wool supplied by the Emperor for this purpose; in most cases this work would have been carried out by the wife. When necessary, women carried heavy loads for their husbands, also the basic chores if the husband was away serving in the mit'a, while the community was responsible for working the family's land.

Inspectors saw that the women kept their houses neat, looked after food hygienically, supplied their family with clothing and reared their children properly. They also made sure that the girls obeyed their mothers or nurses, and were kept busy about the house. Women of the Inca and curaca classes also had to look after their houses. A principal wife had official duties and tasks like some of the wives of prominent citizens in our own society. She was responsible for the smooth running of the household—for the standard of cooking and quantity of chicha prepared, for cleanliness and entertainments.

Apart from looking after their houses, the married women throughout the empire busied themselves with other tasks, such as spinning and weaving, for their family's needs (31). Even the Inca women surrounded themselves with this work: they would take out their distaff and spin as they conversed. Garcilaso tells us that spinning and twisting as they walked was only done by

31 Domestic spinning could be done whilst walking. The backstrap loom could be tied to a peg or post and the necessary tension for weaving maintained by leaning backwards

common people, but the pallas were accompanied by servants carrying their yarn and distaffs. Thus both the callers and ladies of the house were occupied as they conversed. If a wife of a curaca went to vist a palla of royal blood, she did not take her own work to do, but after the first exchange of conversation she would offer to do some work, and, as a sign of favour, the palla would give her something she was working on for one of her daughters, so as not to place her on a level with the servants. Affability was the reward for humility!

Many royal women led celibate lives under chastity vows that could not be broken in the seclusion of their own houses. Garcilaso tells us these women were called Ocllo (Pure) and that they only visited their families on special occasions, or when people were sick. Such women, some of whom were widows, were greatly respected for their chastity and high-mindedness. Since Garcilaso was writing after the Acllahùasi had been banned, these women may have included former Acllas and Mamacunas after the Spanish conquest.

At the other extreme were the prostitutes. They were outcasts who lived in small huts in the fields outside the villages and towns. Called *pampairuna*, meaning public women 'who lived in the open field', they were tolerated by the Incas since they were considered to be a necessary evil. Any woman seen chatting to one ran the risk of being similarly scorned, shorn in public and repudiated by her husband.

The role of women in the Inca court may seem rather limited from our twentieth-century vantage point, since none of the professions were open to married women, nor did they find many opportunities for sexual freedom. The Emperor's wives (concubines) were kept under close guard and observation by the doorkeepers to ensure they remained pure and faithful. Death was the price that a concubine wife and her companion in adultery had to pay if they were caught. The earlier Inca rulers were less severe in meting out punishments when the young men of the court were implicated, and are reported to have cast a blind eye on what Topa Inca referred to 'as the hot blood of youth' but Huayna Capac was very strict on this point, as well as on all other aspects of law.

Punishment was extremely harsh for a woman who killed her husband: she received the death penalty—hanging by the feet in a public place. Otherwise the laws were similar for both sexes.

OLD AGE AND THE DISABLED

The Inca government saw to it that adults were kept fully occupied; the policy was to create work if there was none rather than have persons with time on their hands getting into mischief. Old age officially started when an adult was no longer able to carry out his full work load, and this usually happened somewhere around the fiftieth year.

Once a man was classified as 'old' he ceased to be a taxpayer and like the sick or disabled he could be supported from the Inca's storehouses while he busied himself in less demanding tasks. The Chunca Camayoc reported the needs of the aged and infirm to their superiors and in turn the old were expected to occupy themselves usefully: collecting brushwood or ichu grass, or catching lice, which they then had to deliver to the group leader. The old people also worked to help their families by doing odd chores around the house, looking after and educating the children.

The deformed and disabled were also given suitable jobs. A task for the blind on the coast was to clean the cotton of seeds and other impurities, and in the highlands they removed maize from the husks. Deaf-mutes were not exempt from the tax-work but the sick were exempt while their illness lasted, as were disabled persons. The disabled, deformed and sick were fed and clothed, like the old people, from the Inca Emperor's storehouses. They were also governed by special laws and regulations. A law concerning those who were born with physical deformities required that persons with similar types of deformation inter-married: The blind were married to the blind, deaf-mutes to deaf-mutes, dwarfs to dwarfs, and so on.

In fact, there seems to have been a place for everyone under the Inca regime, each person receiving their basic needs and sustenance so long as they carried out their tasks so that no one lived from begging. As late as 1560 Garcilaso records that he only saw one indian woman beg and that the indians despised her for this, spitting on the ground before her in contempt—so that she begged only from the Spaniards. Later observations of Cobo's on the treatment of the old and infirm suggests that the breakdown of the Inca economic system seriously affected the position and treatment of the old and weak, to whom neither charity or kindness were shown. He says that the old and sick had their food placed beside them and if they were too ill to feed themselves, no one bothered to help them or encouraged them to eat up.

DISEASE AND CURING

Rowe considers that in Inca belief 'all disease had a supernatural cause, and had to be cured by religious and magical means'. However, some herbal medicines were used for physiological reasons as well as purely magical ones. While curing was an important part of Inca religion a recorded saying of Pachacuti Inca suggests an interest in, and knowledge of, the beneficial properties of plants:

> The physician or herbalist who is ignorant of the virtues of herbs, or who knows the virtues of some but does not seek to know the virtues of all, knows little or nothing. He must work until he knows them all, whether useful or injurious, in order to deserve the title he lays claim to.

In some areas at least of the empire there were tribes who were skilled in the curative powers of local plants, and one of these tribes, the *Collahuayna*, were obliged to act as doctors for the Incas. The secrets of curing were carefully kept within the family and the curers were called *Hampi Camayoc*, 'Medicine Specialist'. Probably most people used herbs for a number of simple cures but resorted to other powers when the treatment was not successful and the illness became more serious. While many of the prevalent European diseases such as smallpox, measles and scarlet fever, were unknown in the New World until the arrival of the Spanish conquerors, there were other widespread local diseases such as syphilis, *verruga* and *uta*. Verruga attacks men and animals, its symptoms being warts, fever and sometimes haemorrhages. Uta is a kind of leprosy which mainly attacks the face.

Medicines were made of simple herbs, and only rarely of compounds: *molle* bark, boiled in water was used on fresh wounds; *chillca*, a leaf from a shrub, relieved painful joints and sprains when it was applied after being heated in an earthenware pot; *sarsaparilla*, grown around the Gulf of Guayaquil, was used to kill pain and relieve syphilitic sores, its roots being boiled to make effective purges.

Purges and bleeding were two of the most common treatments for all kinds of minor ailments. For bleeding, a lancet of obsidian was used and people usually bled themselves standing, by opening the vein nearest the place where the pain was felt, or, to relieve a headache, between the eyebrows on the bridge of the nose. Purgatives were taken as antidotes to 'heaviness and sluggishness', and could be made stronger when they were required as a treatment against worms. Purging by means of a clyster pipe (syringe) was also used for enemas.

Urine was kept in the house for many minor complaints, including washing the baby when it had a fever or even as a medicine. The teeth were cleaned with molle twigs and gums were cared for by roasting the twigs, then splitting and placing them against the gums, 'scaulding them they burnt the flesh sloughs off the gums, revealing a new flesh underneath which is very red and healthy'! *Matecllu* was supposed to be excellent for the eyes and could be eaten raw. Mashed, the juice was poured on the ailing eye and the crushed herb placed like a plaster on the eyelids with a bandage to keep it in place. Tobacco or *sairi*, inhaled as a powder helped clear the head, mixed with salt-petre it acted on stone in the liver, and, taken with hot water it cured the retention of urine. Today, all sorts of herbs and leaves are still used by the indians to cure minor ailments. Apart from its action as a stimulant or a pain killer in the form of cochaine, *coca* leaves stop diarrhoea and its juices dry up ulcers. Quinua leaves relieve swelling of the throat, and yucca (mandioc) leaves boiled with salt are placed on joints to help relieve pains from rheumatism. Massages were carried out with animal fats and herbs. Abortions could be achieved by massaging the fetus.

Superstitions made up many of the cures. Sick babies sucked

their umbilical cords which were specially preserved for this purpose; in this way the pain was 'sucked' out of the body, evil spirits and foreign bodies expelled and the body cleansed. When a person gave way to illness he or she called in the local curers, the *Camasca* or *Soncoyoc*, old people with knowledge of plants who could simulate extrasensory powers derived from some vision or extraordinary recovery from illness. They attempted to cure with words and superstitious actions and remedies. While these might prove psychologically beneficial they were often worse than useless physiologically.

Sacrifices played an important role in healing. The sick made their own sacrifices with the assistance of the priests, and, if these proved not to be effective, the Camasca or Soncoyoc was called in, who first sacrificed to his own vision and then attempted to divine the cause of the disease. When the sickness was thought to be due to religious neglect a mixture of black and white maize flour and ground seashells was placed in the hand of the sick person who was ordered to repeat certain words, blow the powder in the direction of the deities. He then offered a little coca to the Sun and scattered bits of gold and silver for Viracocha, the creator. Sickness thought to be caused by neglect of ancestor worship was counteracted with food and chicha, set by the ancestor's tomb, or before the possessions of the deceased in some part of the house.

A cleansing cure which consisted of washing the patient with water and white maize flour at the juncture point of two rivers was prescribed only if the sick person could get there; otherwise he was washed in the home. A noble or person of some wealth who was believed to be suffering from an internal disorder underwent a special cure. This took place in a small room which was first purified by the curer, who cleansed it with black maize flour, burning some and then repeating this with white maize flour. Next, the sick person was placed in the room and was drugged or hypnotized. The curers then opened his stomach with an obsidian knife and cleaned it, pretending to remove snakes, toads and other foreign bodies. Sometimes when a man was very sick and all else had failed, he might even be prepared to sacrifice one of his young children in an attempt to win the approval of the spirits.

Broken bones and dislocations were treated by sacrifices made on the spot where the breakage occurred, since it was considered that these were caused by the place spirits. However, war wounds such as a cracked skull required the services of a skilled surgeon. Trepanning operations may have been performed on such casualties as well as for religious reasons. There appears to have been two methods used in the Cuzco region, examples of which have been found on skulls discovered in cemeteries. One method involved drilling an oval row of small overlapping holes, each about half a centimetre (a quarter of an inch) in diameter. The second method was by sawing two parallel sets of lines which crossed at approximately right-angled corners. The patient was certainly drugged for the operation. That such operations were often successful is borne out by the skulls found, where healing had taken place after several large operations had been performed.

Curers, doctors, surgeons and sorcerers were rewarded and paid with clothes, food, gold and silver, or llamas.

The sorcerers who practised black magic were feared by the Inca and other Andean peoples, especially since they were experts in poisons. They worked suggestively, using human teeth, hair, and nails, as well as figurines, amulets, shells, and parts of animals and toads. Special preparations were strategically placed to cause the 'enemy' maximum disquiet and suffering, in the hope of making him sick or of ruining his crops. Figurine likenesses were also viciously mutilated. However, since a sorcerer convicted of causing death of a person was executed with all his descendants, they probably used some discretion. Sorcerers also furnished love charms.

The prevention of disease was considered a serious matter by the Incas who devised a special ceremony called *Citua*, the purpose of which was to drive sickness and evil from Cuzco. The Citua feast was celebrated in late August or September since at this time

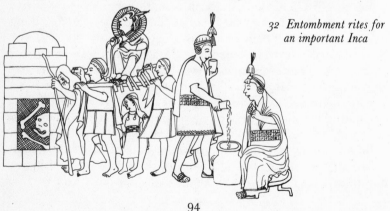

32 Entombment rites for an important Inca

of year the first rains fell, causing many illnesses. All foreigners were evicted from Cuzco before the festival began. In the centre of the town one hundred warriors lined up to face each of the four quarters. The festival began when the high priest of the Sun came out of the Sun Temple. He was greeted by the cry 'Away with evil' by all those present. The warriors then ran in the direction of the quarter they were facing, until they reached others waiting who took over from them, outside the city. Other warriors who did not belong to the population of Cuzco carried the message on to others, and so on until the evil was cast away into a river.

DEATH

A person's death often focused more attention on his or her life, than at any time during their lives, especially in the case of a commoner. The mourning period was quite long—a full year among the nobles. Relatives wore black and the women cut their hair wearing cloaks over their heads and smudging their faces with black paint. No fires were lit in the house until the funeral rites, which lasted for five to eight days, were over. Relatives who attended the funeral were served with food and drink and the mourners did a slow dance accompanied by muffled drums. Following the funeral of an important man (32) pilgrimages were made to places associated with him and songs were sung recounting his successes. A year after the death the mourning period ended with the Cullu Huacani ritual.

Although there was no belief in reincarnation there was an expectation of continued life elsewhere and it was believed that virtuous individuals went to live with the Sun in the upper world '*Hanac-paca*', while sinners went to the interior of the earth to suffer cold and hunger. This did not prevent individuals' souls remaining in some contact with their descendants, who looked after their bodies. Burials therefore consisted of some accommodation for the body of the deceased (p.137) in which he or she was placed in a seated position, wrapped in their best clothes and mats or sewed into a skin. Items buried with the body included pottery, baskets, jewellery, food and the tools of his trade: a fisherman was accompanied by his fishing gear; a warrior by his weapons. Other belongings were burnt or used for the pilgrimages.

Some tombs may have been family burial places. Important Incas and curacas might also have been accompanied by their favourite wives and servants, as in the case of the Emperor.

5

Conquest and Integration

In the Andean area there had already been well over 1,000 years of intermittent warfare, in periods of territorial and personalized frictions between small local groups, and more highly organized conquest drives apparently associated in the first place with religious ideas, which were forced on the areas dominated, as in the case of the Huari-Tiahuanaco expansion in the Middle Horizon.

In their Early period, the *Inca* had successfully carried out raids in local territories and had consolidated these into a state, when the Chanca threatened Cuzco. Perhaps without the threat of this historic attack, the Inca army would never have become large enough, or powerfully enough directed by a sense of purpose to defeat the Chanca and extend their territory into an empire. But having followed up the Chanca defeat with a number of highly successful battles in enemy territory, it seemed as if there was nothing to hold the Incas from extending their conquests indefinitely, until (in their concept) 'the whole world' became theirs. Thus a campaign which had started out in defence of the homeland was transformed into a triumphal conquest drive, made possible by an army largely made up of allies. In return the allies received a place in the new organization of Cuzco, in the empire, and a share of the increasing prestige of the Incas. In this way the continued engagements and successes of the Inca army must have done much to integrate the *Inca* with their new allies and first subjects, who shared in the victories. But it cannot have been only to please their allies that the later Incas continued expanding the empire until it reached its climax in the reign of Huayna Capac.

In the traditional accounts of Inca history the Incas saw themselves as 'bearers of civilization' to 'barbarians', who were incorporated into the Inca system for their own good. Certainly some of the areas conquered and integrated into the empire had little economic advantages to attract the Incas. Although they spread the worship of their 'ancestor the Sun' as the main state religion throughout the empire, the Incas can hardly be described as religious crusaders. The introduction of their religious ideas can be seen more in the light of an education and indoctrinations, through ritual, into Inca customs and organization. Particularly important was the relationship of religious ritual to the economy, of the solar year to the agricultural year (p. 148).

The Inca's policy was to keep the population busy with allotted tasks from which there was little time for subjects to get up to mischief. While some conquests were planned mainly to occupy the Inca army, keeping ambitious generals from plotting internal intrigues, others were intended to stop outsiders harrassing borders or trying to stir up revolts. Service in the army was not necessarily an unattractive proposition; on the contrary, it provided many commoners with their only opportunity to travel and the possibility of reward and advancement in civilian life. The aristocracy also sought their 'fortunes' and often started their careers by distinguishing themselves on active duty in the army.

33 Army dress and weapons: Chinchaysuyu general with his standard. Inca warriors fighting the enemy with clubs and lances

ORGANIZATION OF THE ARMY

Army organization was similar in its pyramidal hierarchy to the civil and political organization. Every ten warriors formed a unit ordered by a native leader—a sergeant responsible for the discipline and daily existence of his group. He was called *Chunga-camayoc* (Guardian of ten). His duties were to see that his men were provided with army dress, arms and supplies, and it was up to him to guide them through foreign territory and train them for war. Every five groups of ten were under a *Picha Chunga-camayoc* (Guardian of 50) who oversaw the activities of the Chunga-camayocs, and inspected them. These in turn were under the command of a *Pachaca Camayoc* and so on, as set out below:

Chungacamayoc	Guardian of 10
Pichca Chungacamayoc	Guardian of 50
Pachaca Camayoc	Guardian of 100
Guaranga Camayoc	Guardian of 1,000
Apu	Captain (of 2,500)
Apuratin	Vice Captain (of 2,500)
Hatun Apu	Commander (of 5,000)
Hatun Apuratin	Vice Commander (of 5,000)
Apusquipay	Commander-in-Chief
Apusquiprantin	Aide to Commander-in-Chief

The two lowest posts in the hierarchical scale were usually held by the camayocs, local civilian officials, who being taxpayers were therefore required to enter one of the services anyway for a spell. Other posts were probably filled largely by professionals, who may not have held civil administrative posts prior to their army experience, but who would almost certainly acquire one when they retired from active duty. Many of these army officials must also have had private lands awarded to them by the Emperor for their service in the army, to which they could retire. Native generals and captains often maintained their rank and commanded their own people under other generals or the Commander-in-Chief of Inca blood set over them. The Emperor and his supreme council chose an experienced military man as chief of the armies. When possible the choice was an uncle or brother of the reigning Inca, or he was a near relative.

Most able-bodied males were trained in the use of arms from boyhood, and could expect to be called up to do their military service sometime between the ages of 25 and 50. The only standing army was the Emperor's, which consisted of a bodyguard of several thousand warriors, and captains of the Inca nobility. When the army was enlisted, each province was requested to send a contingent under a local general. Depending on the locality of the war, these then went to Cuzco to receive their orders or they remained ready to join the main army when it marched near their territory. During Pachacuti Inca's reign 70,000 men fought in the early campaign, led by the unfortunate Capac Yupanqui. Soon after this success the Incas fielded 200,000 men against the Colla and then 250,000 for Topa Inca's great northern campaign.

PREPARATION FOR CONQUEST

Huayna Capac's enlistment for the Quito campaign is well recorded. Having consulted his council and the oracles by the divination ceremony of *Calpa* (p. 194), the Sapa Inca discussed the coming campaign with his generals and the nobles of Cuzco—many of whom offered to accompany him. He then appointed a noble called Mihi as the Commander-in-Chief of Hurin Cuzco, and his own brother Auqui Toma as Commander-in-Chief of Hanan Cuzco. Meanwhile he ordered all the southern contingents to come to Cuzco. When the soldiers arrived they reported for duty, carrying their traditional arms and dressed in their regional costumes. They camped in tents under surveillance, outside the city on hillsides, where they were entertained with food and drink. Here they also received additional army issue and supplies, and rested until their marching orders came. The Incas were careful not to permit too large an army to collect near their capital.

Provincial squadron by provincial squadron, the Collasuyus, Antisuyus and Cuntisuyus, were despatched along the royal road to Quito, encamping and feeding at the *tambos* and storehouses every night. The march was highly disciplined, organized by *Rumancha* (signal men) who could be easily recognized by their insignia. Soldiers who broke ranks to steal food, or molest civilians, did so under pain of death. Each squadron had its standard, a small square banner about 20 centimetres (8 in.) across, painted stiff with insignia and carried on the end of a spear. The soldiers wore their usual costumes, or body armour consisting of quilted cotton tunics, but no cloaks. Helmets, which replaced headdresses were made of quilted cotton or of wood, or were caps of plaited cane. The helmets often had some decoration running across the top from ear to ear. Many soldiers wore woollen fringes below each knee and around their ankles; also, round metal discs were worn, both front and back (*33*). These discs were military awards, the rank of the award being indicated by the type of metal, either bronze, silver, or gold. Although small, these may have occasionally shielded the wearer from the odd blow. Inca soldiers hung round shields of protective armour on their backs, made of hard chonta-palm slats and cotton. On their arms they carried square or round shields made of wooden boards, covered with deerskin or metal, and over these hung a cloth decorated with a painted or woven emblem. In addition, a long shawl or cloth was worn and this could be used as a shield wrapped around the arm, or even wrapped around the body for protection. Captains and generals wore rich and colourful uniforms and were recognized in battle by their plumed helmets.

The Inca contingents were the last to leave Cuzco amid great festivities, after solemn celebrations and sacrifices had taken place before the stone of war in the main plaza, the Huacapata. In special ceremonies designed to lessen the powers of the enemy idols, the priests walked around a fire on which wild birds had been sacrificed (*34*). They carried stones on which snakes, toads, pumas, and jaguars had been carved or painted, chanting: 'May it succeed' and 'May the idols of our enemies lose their strength'. Dark-coloured llamas, prepared by enforced fasting, were then sacrificed. Their hearts were inspected to see if any of the surrounding flesh had been affected and consumed in the

34 Ceremonial bowl carved in stone, since the bowl shows remarkable similarity in shape to the warclub head fig. 38, it is likely that it was used in military rituals

fast; this signified that the hearts of their enemies would similarly grow weak and faint. The participants fasted all day, feasted at night, and danced the taqui with a great cable, the *muru-urca* chain. When the Incas were finally ready to leave Cuzco, they were accompanied by certain idols, representing ancestors— usually stones representing Manco and Huanacauri. With the warrior's morale thus boosted, and with the blessing of the priests, the army marched out from the plaza, in this case taking the Chinchaysuyu road.

When the Emperor accompanied the army, he travelled in his litter among the *Auquicona* (his nearest kin, the highest nobility of Hanan Cuzco), including some of his sons. Other battalions consisted of the *Mancopchurincuzcos* (the 'stem' of the Incas), the *Cacacuzcos* (illegitimate Inca 'stem'), and the *Ayllucuzcos* (Incas by privilege). The battalions and squadrons from Chinchaysuyu joined the Inca army, falling in behind it as it marched northward through their territory.

With the aid of strategically placed lodges and supply bases the armies could be quickly and easily moved up along the main roads. The stops were spaced at about 20 kilometres (12 miles) throughout subdued territories. Conquests of new provinces were carefully prepared for by building roads and tambos nearby, (*35, 36*) or as far into the enemy territory as possible, before

35 Inca road stop near Cusichaca

36 Important royal stopping place with fountains at Tambo Machai near Cuzco

engaging in serious battle. When this was not possible the army had to rely on supplies carried by men and thousands of llamas. In some instances special bridges of access had to be improvised and built (p. 139). The Incas also ordered fortresses or fortified towns built to accommodate the army and supplies during a prolonged seige (37).

Before starting a conquest the Emperor sent ambassadors and spies into those provinces and territories he planned to occupy or pass through. The army did not necessarily win all its victories in battles, some were won by sheer diplomacy. Upon the advance of the enormous Inca army many of the smaller tribes and provinces recognized that it was useless to resist. Instead they listened to the Sapa Inca's envoys, who assured them that it was advantageous to become the Inca's subjects, to embrace the religion of the Sun and enjoy an ordered and civilized existence. Furthermore, the envoys promised them, no harm would be done to those who became their subjects without resistance; on the contrary, certain privileges and immunities would be granted them and their leaders would not lose their position or authority. In this way Topa Inca's great campaigns were considerably speeded up.

37 *Paramonga fortress on the north coast. Photograph of a model in the Museo Nacional de Antropologia, Lima*

FIGHTING

Large provinces, and some smaller ones able to make alliances with their neighbours, resisted the Incas. The Inca army's advantages lay in its numbers, its well-organized supply and communications systems, which enabled it to survive without camp followers, and its range of weapons. The army could rely on a great variety of both close- and long-range weapons, since contingents from different provinces were expert at fighting with their traditional weapons, developed in a variety of conditions. For instance, the Colla were specialists in the use of the *ayllus* (*bolas*, made of three stones tied to cords or thongs which were united in one cord, excellent when thrown, for entangling the legs of men or animals); the Antisuyus, forest indians, were experts in the use of the bow and arrow; and the Ecuadorian and coastal tribes used spear and dart throwers. The sling, called *huaraca*, was universally used and was worn by the soldiers tied around their waists like belts. Varieties of clubs were also popular among the Andeans. The soldiers carried both their native arms and some of those supplied by the Incas. The Incas fought mainly with clubs and spears, the most popular being a star-headed mace, a club with a circular head of stone or metal with six projecting

38 Stone Inca warclub; similar shaped clubs were also made of cast bronze

points set in a wooden handle of about 80 centimetres (32 in.) length (*38*). The *macana* was a sword-shaped club made of hard black chonta-palm wood, about 1.2 metres (4 ft) long and 10 centimetres (4 in.) wide, tapering towards a handgrip which was rounded and ended in a knob (*34*). Battleaxes and halberds of stone and bronze heads were used on shafts of various lengths. Also used were simple spears: long poles with fire-hardened points or metal tips, although in later times they were probably employed more often in rituals than in actual battle.

Martial music played an important part in the battle scene: in boastful songs the Incas proclaimed their prowess and insulted the enemy. Tambourines, probably covered with the skins of past enemies, and bone flutes were played. Trumpets of shell and clay were blown as signals in the heat of battle. The music, the sheer numbers of men and the colourful brilliance of an Inca army must have been an awesome experience for the enemy. The Emperor, when he accompanied an army, remained in his litter with the royal standard, surrounded by his bodyguard of over 1,000 warriors. His vulnerability on such occasions is well documented in Inca history: in a battle with the Caranquis a surprise attack caught the Incas unprepared so that they scattered; then, seeing Huayna Capac fall from his litter, his bodyguard fled, thinking he was dead. Fortunately another battalion, the Yanacona (the Inca's personal servants) saw him and saved him. It was not wise for an all-powerful Emperor to be caught in the midst of fighting, and in the case of Huascar Inca it proved fatal, since once he was ambushed and captured he lost the empire to Atahuallpa.

Fighting was begun at long range, by the slingers. Closer in, the bowmen fired their arrows, and finally when the two sides closed, the-hand-to-hand fighters with their clubs and spears brought the battle to a climax. Most soldiers used only one offensive weapon at a time, using their shields to defend themselves. Although the Incas had superiority of numbers, in a pitched battle this advantage was lessened with the breakdown of discipline and loss of command once the armies had closed. Each man fought for himself, boasting and shouting in the heat of the battle: 'They give their mouths no rest when they are fighting', wrote one chronicler. It was due to this confusion that the Inca's personal security was threatened. However, strategy played an important role and the Incas often made good use of this confusion to capture an enemy leader or cult object, thus demoralizing the other side. Another favourite device was to divide their forces into three armies: one army would engage the enemy to assess its strength before calling in the other forces in surprise flank attacks. A further device in pitched battle was to set fire to the grass scrub around an enemy located in a strong position.

In the highlands, the inhabitants of a resisting province usually withdrew, barricading themselves into well-chosen hilltop fortresses, on which the battle would then focus. These defenders of a hill fort or a mountain pass would then roll large boulders down on the approaching enemy. Both defenders and attackers used slings of plaited wool, ichu grass, or rawhide which propelled stones the size of eggs. Cieza records that the Incas knew how to prepare the stones by heating them and coating them with flaming bitumen and aiming them at enemy thatched roofs. They usually refrained, however, from indiscriminate burning of enemy towns unless their patience had been exhausted. Also, they forbade the use of poison on the tips of weapons. In attacking a fortress the Incas protected themselves from the hail of enemy sling stones by using great sheets of tough cotton, each of which covered about 100 men.

Since hilltop fortresses were effectively constructed on steep slopes with many surrounding terraces, and walls with salient sections (39), the Incas usually preferred to cut the enemies off from their supplies and wait: the coastal states were particularly vulnerable to such methods. Also, their water supplies could be cut off and diverted, at their source in the highlands. Other methods of dealing with enemy fortresses depended on enticing them out. We are told that Incas accomplished this in their war against the Caranquis in Quito, by using their favourite device of dividing the army into three forces: one part of the army pretended to weaken and flee, and when the enemy left their stronghold to pursue them, another branch of the army came up from behind, to cut off their retreat. Meanwhile, the third part of the army entered the undefended fortress. The enemy also played tricks. Pretending to succumb to a blockade, they thus invited the Inca army into their fort only to surprise them in a trap.

VICTORY

Important prisoners and trophies were taken in battle. But during the fighting there was no incentive for taking prisoners at random; this was not the point of the battle (as for instance it was with the Aztecs). When an important enemy was killed in battle his head might be made into a trophy cup. This was done by fitting the head with a metal cup in the crown. Drums too were constructed of enemy skins—the skin was flayed, stuffed with straw and ashes and the stomach part was used for the drum head. Inca soldiers also sometimes made their bone flutes with an enemy's shin-bone, and necklaces of their teeth. However, once defeated, the enemy was not maltreated and after the Incas had taken their choice of captives to Cuzco for a triumphal entry, most of them

39 The greatest of the Inca fortresses, Sacsahuaman, had three enormous zig-zagging lines of defensive terracing, see also plan of Cuzco, page 114

were allowed to return to a normal life at home, or elsewhere, except that they were now Inca subjects.

After an important conquest, a triumphal entry into Cuzco was carefully organized. The triumph might last several days. The army would display its trophies, booty and prisoners of war, sing victory songs and accounts of the battles. Examples of everything found on the conquest which would most impress the citizens of Cuzco, were displayed through the streets. Several thousand captives chosen from among the most representative men, women and children of their province were shown off. Prisoners were made to lie prostrate in the Temple of the Sun while the Emperor symbolically trod on their backs or necks declaiming 'On my enemies I step'. These ceremonies were followed by sacrifices, dancing the taqui and feasting. A few of the more important or dangerous leaders might be sacrificed, or executed in a sub-terranean prison filled with dangerous animals or snakes (p. 133). The rest of the prisoners were then sent home, or, if they belonged to a particularly troublesome province, were later sent with their families to new lands as *mitimaes* (p. 109). Unmarried captive women were divided up among the army captains and generals or were kept by those who had captured them. The army then received its awards and was disbanded.

Awards consist of gifts of clothing, gold, and silver-plate pendants. However, the gift of a chosen woman for a wife, a hereditary post in the administration, or a gift of land were the marks of the Emperor's favour. Nobles were rewarded with luxury gifts, wives, promotion, or they were granted special privileges such as travelling in a litter, or sitting on a stool— luxuries only permitted to those with special licence.

ORGANIZATION OF CONQUERED PROVINCES

After the army subjected a province, the quipucamayocs and engineers were sent in to assess the resources of the new territory. The quipucamayocs made a census of the population so that each householder was entered and all his dependants categorized according to their age groups. Rowe points out that the Incas made 12 standard age divisions for tax assessment and that, although the precise age of a person was not recorded, their physical condition was assessed for classification. Engineers surveyed the territories making calculations of the arable lands, the crops grown, and sought out sources for metals (copper, tin, gold and silver) that could be mined. Painted clay models were constructed for the government, showing settlements and their geographical environments with amazing accuracy. These models and the census quipus were then taken to Cuzco, with the conquering general's report, where they were presented to the Emperor. The information concerning each province was then studied by the Emperor and his advisers, before decisions were made for reorganizing the population and increasing the arable acreage, where this was desirable.

For the administration of a new province, the Emperor appointed a provincial governor responsible only to him and the Apucuna of the quarter. The governor, or *Tocricoc Apu*, resided in the local capital from which he governed the province in the Emperor's name. The choice was made from ranks of the Incas of royal blood, who might include the general involved in the conquest of the province. The Tocricoc Apu(s) were given special privileges such as the right of travelling on a litter, using household utensils of gold and silver, and generally living in sufficient luxury to impress the native population.

The local curacas and chiefs retained their positions in the new administration so long as they carried out the Emperor's demands in implementing Inca customs and laws. The curacas had to send their sons to Cuzco as hostages for their good behaviour, where they received an education which prepared them for administrative posts in the empire. The most important idols and deities belonging to the native populations of provinces were removed to Cuzco, as additional insurance against rebellion. This was especially effective in the Andean area, since there was great significance attached to the power of idols and it was believed that if they fell into foreign hands, this power could be used against their previous owners. To mitigate the effect of this law the Incas permitted native priests and embassies to accompany and serve their idols in the place where they were kept.

The Incas were usually at pains to win the support of their new subjects and their native leaders, whom they sought to please with gifts of gold and silver, or by awarding them special privileges that would honour them and increase their prestige in the eyes of their followers, The natives of the province were then instructed in the tribal emblems that they were obliged to wear, and in the style of their headbands or headdresses. They were also instructed in Quechua, and in the religion of the Sun, to which they were ordered to give priority of worship, in deference to the divine ancestry of the Incas. They were permitted to continue worshipping their native deities and idols so long as the attention they gave them did not interfere with the Sun's supremacy. The Incas, in turn, sometimes made gifts to local shrines and listened to the more famous of their oracles. The famous pre-*Inca* oracle of Pachacamac, on the coast, sensibly 'agreed' to share its prestige with the Temple of the Sun built next to it; in turn, it became one of the most revered temples in the empire and its oracle was consulted by the Sapa Inca himself in making important decisions.

MITIMAES

Under the Inca system of *mitimaes* (colonists), the most troublesome sections of a population were resettled in other territories amongst older and more loyal subjects. These exchanges were carefully studied. The Incas took great pains to see to it that areas of similar climate, economy and altitude were chosen.

There were three types of mitimaes in the Inca period. The oldest, traditional Andean type, was created for economic reasons: local groups were sent by their curaca into a foreign province of a different geographical zone, in order to acquire a greater range of food products in the homeland (p. 141). These groups were not strictly mitimaes since they were counted in the census as belonging to their original provinces, and they were still responsible to their native curaca. The second type were Quechua-speaking 'Incas by privilege', who were special privileged mitimaes, sent to live in the subject capitals and provincial Inca settlements. They were expected to support the Inca administration, set a good example and indoctrinate the locals into the Inca customs and language. The third type of mitimaes were those referred to above, who were the troublesome or rebellious elements in the population—resettled for security reasons in underpopulated provinces, or among loyal subjects.

PLANNING

First, roads of access were built into a new province; these were then lined with tambos and storehouses, stocked with supplies for the government officials, the public works force, the travelling mitimaes, and all those who were in need after a seige. Small posts for runners, called *Chasqui* Posts, were built beside the

40 *Chasqui relay runner blowing on a conch meets a road official*

road at intervals of approximately every 2 or 3 km (1 or 2 miles) (*35, 40*). These formed an efficient communications network throughout the empire, so that if there was an uprising or any disturbance in the province, the news reached the Emperor rapidly (p. 137). When they were needed, engineers, specialized in building canals and irrigation works, were sent in to increase the acreage under cultivation. Terraces, also, were sometimes built on the slopes at the valley sides (p.142).

The Emperor and his advisers then chose a suitable site for the new capital of the province. Usually a site was selected with good visibility and a large level area, which was as near as possible to the old capital, or town. Since many of the pre-Incas had lived in small unplanned towns or in forts located in high inaccessible places, it was the objective of the Inca government to find more convenient positions, nearer roads of access, for re-settlement (*41*). Populations in the highlands were therefore transferred to the valleys; small towns or villages were in many cases built for them, with their cooperation, on the lower slopes just above the level under cultivation, and near a water supply. The mit'a work force was sent into a province to help with the building of the towns and other building works: this consisted of a veritable army of workers who were sent by the government wherever they were needed (p. 159).

In some areas of the empire integration was easily achieved, in others it was difficult to enforce. For instance, the already highly organized coastal states such as the Chimu were integrated with the Inca administration with little alteration, especially since the Incas had already borrowed many of their more advanced ideas on organization. In the case of the eastern

41 Planning: terraced landscape and settlements on Pisac mountain

provinces of the jungle zone, the opposite was true. The Incas found it almost impossible to integrate these areas more than partially into the empire, due to the geographical barriers and to the extremely different life style of the forest tribes. In many cases those tribes who were unwilling to become vassals abandoned their villages.

One of the more commendable qualities of the Incas was that wherever they encountered ideas and practices they considered had some merit they were prepared to utilize them, or permit them to continue. When the Chimu were conquered, the Incas were so impressed with their organization that the king and some of their finest craftsmen were brought to live in Cuzco so that the Incas might learn from them.

6

Life in the capital
and provincial towns

Cuzco is situated at 3,560 metres (11,600 ft) above sea level and
some 13½ degrees south of the equator. It occupies a site at the
head of a mountain valley with a temperate climate, cool when
it rains and cold at night. Cuzco was a small village up to the
time of the Chanca threat, after which it became the political
and religious capital of the expanding Inca empire. Today it is the
third town of Peru, overlying and still incorporating parts of the
original Inca capital. As the Inca capital, Cuzco was replanned by
Pachacuti Inca, after 1440, with a new centre to the north of the
old nucleus, obtained by draining a previous swamp area.
Unfortunately, few Spanish eyewitness descriptions were written
before the Incas themselves destroyed the city by burning in
1535.

The city was designed by Pachacuti as a metropolis, representing the four quarters of the empire. He ordered two small rivers,
the Huatanay and Tullumayo, to be canalized: between these,
all the most important buildings of Cuzco proper were built.
That the inner city of Cuzco was laid out in the shape of a puma
has now been well established by Chavez Ballon and Rowe (see
Bibliography). The fortress of *Sacsahuaman*, built in the north,
overlooking the main body of the town, represents the puma's
head, and the ward called *Pumacchupan* (Puma's tail) which contained the botanical gardens, is located in the lower, southern-
most section where the two rivers unite (*43*:10). The inner city
covered an area between the two rivers of about 2,000 metres
(2,150 yds) by 400–600 metres (440–650 yds), and was estimated
by one chronicler to have contained about 4,000 structures. The
buildings were arranged in wards separated by narrow streets.

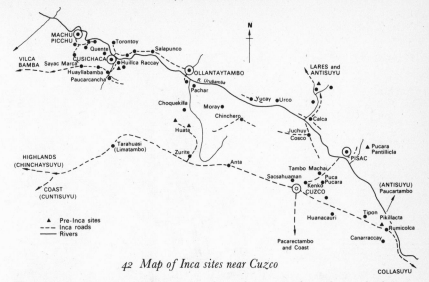

42 *Map of Inca sites near Cuzco*

The wards were approximate quadrangles, sometimes irregularly shaped since the normally straight streets were irregular where the topography interfered. The streets were paved, and water was distributed and drained in small stone-lined channels along their centres.

The heart of this new city was in *Huacapata* (Holy Place), the central plaza, which covered about ten acres. The Huacapata, located in the main body of the puma was where the Incas celebrated important events and held occasions of state. From the corners of the square each of the four great roads led diagonally to the four quarters. Adjacent to the Huacapata and extending from it, there was a secondary ceremonial plaza, the *Cusipata* (Joy Place), which was reached by a flight of steps: this occupied a space of about 4,000 square metres (5,000 sq. yds) between the puma's front and back legs, was paved with pebbles, and was where social gatherings took place. Throughout the empire it was a general rule that all activities should take place in the open: the large ceremonial plazas at the centres of towns were therefore places where the entire population could gather for important occasions and banquets. Some plazas were also used for markets.

The greatness of the city of Cuzco was displayed in its impressive palaces, which apart from their royal function were variously administrative, religious and academic centres. Most of them were built of finely fitted, dressed masonry, although

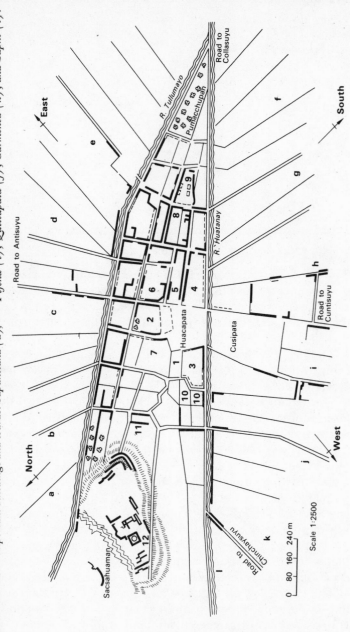

43 Plan of the Inca capital, Cuzco, as organized by Pachacuti Inca in the shape of a puma. (After Dr. M. Chavez Ballon) Numbers 1–12 = important buildings and wards. Sapantiana (a), Quantu Pata (b), Tococachi (c), Munay Sanca (d), Rimac Pampa (e), Coripata (f), Cayaocachi (g), Chaquilchaca (h), Pijchu (i), Quillapata (j), Carmenca (k), and Saphi (l).

sometimes partially of adobe (sun-dried bricks); the roofs were always thatched, sometimes with great ingenuity and decorative elaboration, and interiors were often generously ornamented with gold and silver. The palaces were built around the central plaza and each contained one or more quadrangles. This basic Cuzco plan was established by Pachacuti Inca, and was adapted for use elsewhere. Around the Huacapata were the palaces of the Hanan Cuzco Incas (*43*), including those of the four Emperors: These were *Cora-cora* 1, palace of Inca Roca; *Quishuarcancha* 2, the Temple or palace of Viracocha Inca; *Cassana* 3, the palace of Pachacuti Inca (Pachacuti is also reported to have occupied other palaces and a 'hut' in Cora-cora); *Hatuncancha* or *Pucamarca* 6, located next to the Acllahuasi 5, was the palace of Topa Inca; *Amarucancha* 4 was the palace of Huayna Capac; Huascar Inca's palace was next to Cora-cora, no. 7 on the plan *43*.

The chroniclers vary somewhat in their attribution of palaces to particular Incas. One Inca, as in the case of Pachacuti Inca, may have had several palaces, used at different periods during his lifetime. Other important buildings off the Huacapata were the *Acllahuasi* 5, House of the Sun Virgins and Chosen Women, and the *Yachahuasi* school for nobles (10).

The Sun Temple, *Coricancha* (Enclosure of Gold), became the most important religious building in the empire when it was rebuilt on a larger scale, on its original site in Hurin Cuzco 9, to the southeast of the new centre. It occupied the most prominent position in Hurin Cuzco, while the great fortress of Sacsahuaman dominated the town from a hill on the northern side. The town itself was not fortified or enclosed with a great wall; instead the fortress of Sacsahuaman was built to provide a place of refuge, with extensive accommodation and storage facilities (12).

In addition to the main temples of Cuzco proper, Coricancha (Temple of the Sun), Quishuarcancha (Temple of Viracocha, the Creator) and Illapa (Temple of the Thunderbolt in the Pucamarca palace), the Incas maintained many shrines and also kept a principal idol from each province in the Coricancha. In the Inca religious system (see Ceque System, p. 189), there was an idol or shrine for every day of the year, represented in an appropriate geographical position in relation to its neighbours, in the environs of the capital.

Only the rulers and Inca nobility (including the priests and important government officials) resided permanently in Cuzco.

44 Rumicolca, the tollgate marking the southern entrance to the valley

Some servants and attendants to the shrines may have lived there temporarily, but many lived in outlying districts. Outside the central nucleus of the 'Puma' city, there were other settlements, or suburbs, which were considered parts of the capital.

Suburbs like these incorporated residences of the native lords of the provinces, where they were required to live for four months of each year maintaining a permanent embassy and servants. Such embassies were distributed around the capital in an order based on the layout of the provinces within the geography of the empire. Incas by privilege also lived in the suburbs and in settlements near Cuzco, some of which may have been their original homes.

The outlying buildings, which were constructed mainly of stone and mud mortar, were not as finely built as those of the inner city: some had upper storeys of adobe bricks, others might even have been built entirely of adobe bricks, covered with a mud stucco finish. The King of Spain's inspector said there were 100,000 of these houses and that they were painted red or yellow. This figure may have been intended to apply to the whole of the valley, which was full of small settlements, connected with Cuzco by paved roads, canalized streams crossed by paving stones, and terraces.

The entrance proper to the Cuzco valley from the south was at Rumicolca, marked by a massive gateway which functioned as a toll-gate, where tribute produce coming into Cuzco was sorted and counted (*42*, *44*). A similar gate must have marked the entrance to Cuzco in the north. These toll-gates were located partly to enforce certain regulations: no one, for instance, might enter Cuzco at night between sunset and sunrise; when entering, the commoners were supposed to do reverence by wearing an additional token burden; no gold, silver, or fine cloth could be taken out of Cuzco, although some exception must have been made for the awards and gifts distributed by the Sapa Inca to his favoured subjects. All provincials (commoners and foreigners) were obliged to leave Cuzco during some of the Incas special ceremonies which took place at certain times of the year. For those who attempted to break these regulations, or who had committed some graver offence, there were two or three kinds of prison in Cuzco. However, most offences were punished immediately (p.133).

The storehouses, where most of the tribute was stored in Cuzco, were located in lines, on a hill overlooking the city from the southwest. Here hundreds of storehouses, belonging to the Sun and to the Inca Emperor, contained many kinds of produce sent in from all over the empire. Produce from those of the Sun supported the priests and attendants of the shrines; and that from the storehouses of the Emperor was used to feed all those inhabitants of Cuzco proper, and those who served in the city. The consumption of food was apparently enormous, especially since all those who lived in the capital were supplied with dried meat from the Emperor's stores. Servants and attendants in the royal service fulfilled a wide range of tasks (p. 159). Several thousand were required to serve an Emperor's palace, and an equivalent number were reported to have served the Coricancha. The royal artisans were also based here, including those who made articles of gold and silver under the Sapa Inca's orders.

PROVINCIAL CAPITALS

The Governors and most of the important Inca representatives lived in the capitals of the provinces. Built by the Incas' public work force, they served as political and religious focal points from which each province could be ruled, and to which tribute could be brought each year before its redistribution.

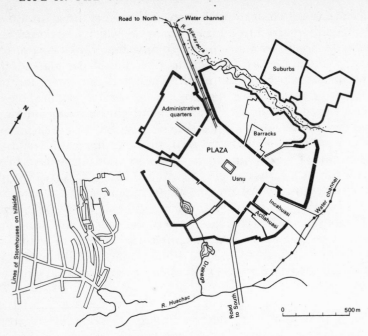

45 *Plan of Huánuco, a highland provincial capital.* (After Harth-Terre)

The layout of the provincial capitals throughout the empire was similar to the basic town plan of Cuzco, although local geographical features and topography were always taken into account and even exploited. The centres of these towns were in their large plazas, where the local population could gather. Here, in each, the Sapa Inca's usnu platform was located, and there were roads in at least three directions. The plazas varied in shape, from square and rectangular forms to irregular trapezoids and an almost triangular shape, depending on the topography.

Huánuco is one of the most complete surviving examples of an Inca administrative capital. Here there was an unusually large usnu set in an enormous central plaza, bounded by the most important government buildings and facilities (45). An important palace and temple of the Incas, called Incahuasi, stood at the eastern side, next to it was located the Acllahuasi, which in size and general plan was remarkably similar to that of the Emperor's palace (52). Religious structures, dominated by the cult of the Sun, were situated at the other end of these two great enclosures, so that the innermost buildings of the royal palace and the Acllahuasi had direct access to the shrines. The Incas by privilege also lived at the centres of the towns, in a series of structures surrounding large courtyards in a regular plan, rather like barracks (49), and the important curacas were represented in the organization of the town with residences which they occupied for part of every year. As in Cuzco, the less prominent members of the organization and society lived further from the centre. Those provincials who lived permanently in the area, farming the surrounding lands, lived in smaller scattered settlements beyond the territory of the capital, in villages often lacking planning and built according to local architectural traditions.

The most important structures, such as the royal palaces and temples in these capitals, were built of finely fitted masonry, and the lesser ones either of stone set in mud mortar and adobe bricks, or entirely of the latter. With or without gables, all buildings were, as in the case of Cuzco, thatched, and streets were paved

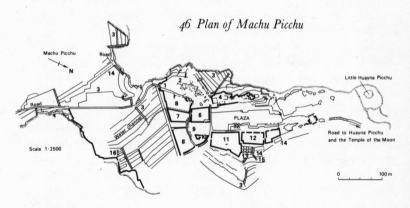

46 Plan of Machu Picchu

1 *City gate*
2 *Burial caves*
3 *Terraces*
4 *Sacred Plaza with the Temple of the Sun, Temple of the Three Windows, and a priest's house*
5 *Intihuatana hill*
6 *Inca palace*
7 *Torreon group*
8 *Residential groups*
9 *Stairway of the fountains*
10 *Religious and all prison facilities*
11 *Ingenuity residence group and garden*
12 *Terraces and houses*
13 *Storehouses*
14 *Large halls*
15 *Beginning of stairway to the cemeteries*
16 *Outer barracks and Posts*

47 Coastal administrative centre. Photograph of a model of Tambo Colorado in the Museo Nacional de Antropologia, Lima

and narrow, with water-channels running along their centres. Like Cuzco, these capitals were not protected by fortifications; instead, a fortress was usually constructed nearby into which the population could conveniently take refuge. Hundreds of storehouses lined the hillsides surrounding the towns, and officials at toll-gates on the main roads of access would check the transportation of tribute and produce.

Besides the politico-religious capital in each province, there were centres of less prestige which catered for purely administrative needs. These lacked the more impressive palace and temple buildings, since they were evidently built entirely for residential and storage purposes.

Provincial capitals and administrative centres of varying importance were all linked together on the road network, the most important capitals being spaced at intervals along the royal roads. In the highlands, from Cuzco to Quito, the most important capitals were: Limatambo, Vilcashuaman, Jauja, Bombon, Huánuco, Huamachuco, Cajamarca, Huancabamba, Ayavaca, Loja, Tomebamba, Llactacunga, Quito and Caranqui. South from Cuzco were: Cacha, Ayaviri, Hatuncolla, Tiahuanaco, Chuquiabo, Chucuito, Paria and others into Chile. Most of these capitals had roads linking them with the coast, via roads which descended into the valleys to the important coastal towns (*47*), and also to settlements and territories of the eastern Andes.

Some important towns, such as Pisac, Ollantaytambo and Machu Picchu (Frontispiece and (46)), occupied prestigious strategic positions in the Inca organization, whether for their strategic importance, for their pleasant climate and situation, or for their religious importance.

In between the capitals and large towns were smaller towns, and between these were the villages, rest-houses, tambos and Chasqui posts, all located at regular intervals (See Chapter 5). Along the coast these facilities were more sparsely spaced since there was virtual desert between the towns built in each river valley. Most travel on the coast was by way of the inland valleys which ran between the coastal and the highland towns. Tribute payments made by coastal towns were sent to highland capitals: the important Chimu province, for instance, sent its tribute payment to Cajamarca, where it was housed until dispatched to Cuzco by the Inca governor.

48 Stone architectural model

ARCHITECTURE AND BUILDING

In the Inca environment, stone represented permanence in an atmosphere where damp did not favour the survival of other materials. Careful stone construction was probably first used in association with agriculture in terracing, which, of necessity, had to be well-fitting to be effective, especially on slopes. It was also used in irrigation schemes. Stone was increasingly used, and by the time the Incas became empire builders, the mit'a labour force was organized to supply the necessary artisans and man-power for an empire style to evolve, based on the use of this material.

Buildings and engineering works, including terraces and irrigation schemes, were carefully designed by architects and engineers from the ranks of the Incas. The plans were worked out in detailed clay models; sometimes stone models were also carved (*48*). The Inca architects and engineers were responsible for all works in the Cuzco region and many of those in other provinces, especially prominent buildings such as the Sun Temples, fortresses and the Inca's palaces. These structures were built of the finest masonry, while others were of inferior quality or partially built of adobe bricks (p. 164). Architecture was a highly respected art since Pachacuti himself was an ardent designer and was referred to as an 'architect' more than once.

Inca measurements were surprisingly consistent, based on the parts of the human body; in taking measurements they used two sticks as a sliding-rule but with arbitrary units of measurement; they also utilized the plumb-bob (*76*,i). However, they were limited in their architecture by certain gaps of knowledge, particularly of geometry. Such limitations, general to the Andean area, were partially overcome by quite simple inventions and contrivances. For instance, the principle of the arch was not mastered but advanced corbelling methods achieved similar ends. Road engineering in the Cuzco area demonstrates a method of bridging culverts, by means of a kind of the corbelled arch, on which the road was later placed. A stone bridge in the Carabaya area shows an advanced use of the corbelled arch over a distance of 10 metres (33 ft). Ordinary buildings in the Cantamarca province achieved several storeys by means of a complicated series of corbelling slabs and narrowing walls, and the Incas demonstrated that they knew of, and could use, this technique in structures on the Island of Titicaca. This corbelled arch, however, was not generally used in large buildings, where perhaps it would have become too complex and overladen.

Architects and engineers were careful about drainage and guarded against the accumulation of ground water. Small channels or conduits were constructed under storehouses, in or under walls of compounds and terraces and wherever pools were likely to collect. Furthermore, such was the skill of the stonemasons in keying or locking a wall by the irregularity of its members that they were able to construct buildings on rock foundations which tilted at angles of up to 40 degrees from the horizontal plane, without using mortar or cement. Ingenious stone-fitting kept granite ashlars keyed together at the point of greatest strain, so that in an earthquake many of these walls could be shaken and lifted and would then settle into position again.

The Incas were not concerned with building vertically, but more in achieving an organic spreading style of architecture, the outstanding characteristics of which were its solidarity and formal simplicity. The trapezoid is the most marked feature of the architecture and was used for many details: for niches of all sizes and in almost all positions in walls; for doorways covered with stone or wooden lintels; also, for most openings and windows in the walls of structures. This extended even to the silhouette of buildings, since the walls inclined inward with the heaviest masonry placed at the bottom. Buildings were invariably one-roomed, and their details were made up of irreducible units, incorporated with symmetrical regularity, into structures of all sizes and types of construction.

The distribution of rectangular structures all over the Inca empire testifies that the canons of Inca architecture favoured this form for individual structures and layouts (although the Chanca and Colla traditionally built round structures). The Incas used the rectangular form wherever the site terrain permitted its use, but the form was not always regular, and corners did not necessarily meet at right angles. When irregularities of terrain, interfering rocks or limited site areas were encountered, the Incas adopted the plan that best fitted the circumstances, using irregular or curved forms. The curved forms were most often used on small sites in the Urubamba drainage.

In towns, two to eight buildings were arranged around court-yards forming compounds to which there were often single entrances. An important palace might consist of a series of such compounds. In small villages the arrangements were often looser and 'extended' families shared compounds, each related family group living in one of the structures. Access to the compound was provided by roads, terraces and stairways paved with stone. Stairways were used particularly in mountain villages, where the groups of houses varied to a greater extent; some might be built in a row, on a single terrace or on two or more terraces, but even here a group was arranged around a central courtyard if space permitted. Courtyards were used for eating, entertainment and other outdoor activities. Sometimes, in a series of compounds, two courtyards might be divided by a

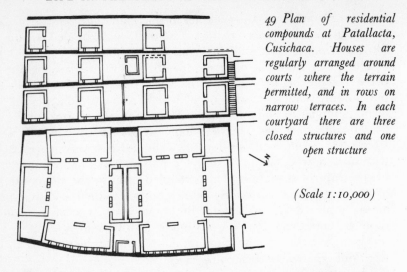

49 *Plan of residential compounds at Patallacta, Cusichaca. Houses are regularly arranged around courts where the terrain permitted, and in rows on narrow terraces. In each courtyard there are three closed structures and one open structure*

(Scale 1:10,000)

50 The 'Ingenuity' residential group at Machu Picchu

double structure. These were not usually constructed side-by-side, like Western semi-detached houses, but back-to-back, sharing a common back wall—each 'house' facing onto a different court-yard (*49, 50*)

Inca buildings varied greatly in size; these variations more often indicated differences in function than in prestige. The largest structures were halls, used for entertainment in bad weather and, when they were required for this purpose, as barracks. The finest temples and palaces consisted of several well-built but modest-sized structures. A basic distinction in function existed between structures with trapezoidal doorways in their front walls (covered by a lintel and masonry), leaving enough space for comfortable entry; and others that had an open, or almost open, front wall, articulated only by the roof timber which traversed the opening. The more closed type of structure, whose doorways did not exceed 1.65 metres (68 in.), were by far the most widely used for habitations and storehouses. The open-fronted structures, with entrances exceeding 2.70 metres (108 in.) were built for daytime activities in the warmer climates, and also sometimes as shrines.

The majority of Inca structures were single-storeyed and few had a full second storey. Some, especially double structures, had attic storeys which were used for storage purposes and were entered from the outside through a window in the gable. Roofs were designed to meet the damp climatic conditions of the highland environment and were sloped to carry off rain. Materials used were often, but not always available locally. Wood for the frame was usually obtainable on the lower slopes of valleys. Ichu grass, used for thatching, could be found on the upper slopes of valleys. This craft was carried out with various degrees of elaboration. Simple thatching with ichu grass continues to the present day. The 'hip' roof was used in one-storeyed rectangular structures: it consisted of a timber frame which rested on the tops of the walls, supporting a thatched roof that sloped on all sides from a central beam. The gable roof was used mainly in two-storeyed or attic-storeyed structures. Vaulted roofs built with the corbelling technique, were rarely used by the Incas except in round chullpas for tombs. On the coast, where the Incas adopted local forms and materials, they also adopted flat roofs on some sites.

The Incas invented a number of small, useful gadgets for tying down roofs, and shutting doorways. 'Eye-bonders' (stones bored with holes) embedded in sloping gable tops were used for tying the roof beams securely in place. These could also be adapted for use on the side of a doorway or niche. Stone pegs projecting on the outside of gable walls were also used for tying the roof in place. Barholds (small niches with cylindrical stone bars placed in them) were used on the outsides of doorways to compounds. A taboo stick could be tied to a barhold to indicate the owner's absence.

ORNAMENTATION AND INTERIORS

Ornamentation, in the form of decorative mouldings, occurs only in rare instances even in coastal sites; where mouldings are found, they are an integral part of a wall structure and are not added to it. In many instances, however, carvings and sculpted rocks may have been closely associated with the architecture. Elaborate decoration, consisting of textiles or gold and silver attachments, were applied to structures and many of these, including stone and mud mortar structures, were stuccoed with mud, at least on the inside, and some were then painted.

There were a few structural elements included for their ornamental effects. Additional jambs, for instance, were the most usual device to articulate important doorways, windows, and niches, and also signified prestige. Double, and even treble jambs, might be used in full-length niches (73) and doorways, and some niches were stepped beneath their lintels. Niches, as well as being functional, were used to create patterns tastefully arranged and integrated in the architectural form. Low-relief carvings occurred but rather infrequently, on outside walls; either as small-scale representations of animals (51) on finely fitted blocks, framing a doorway, or, in rare instances, as carvings in geometric patterns (6). The play of planes is also an important ornamental aspect of Inca architecture and manifests itself in sculpted cave shrines,

51 A puma was carved at each side of the doorways in the Inca's palace, Huánuco

open-air rock carvings and in terracing projects which become veritable sculpted landscape (*71*, *59*). Masonry construction at its finest also fulfilled the aesthetic needs of ornamentation by the play of light on the precision-fitted polygonal and rectangular styles with sunken joints.

There was no furniture as we know it in the interior of houses, except for the low stools that the Incas themselves and other important persons had. In rare instances a stone bench has been found, as for instance at Machu Picchu. A pile of blankets catered generally for both sitting and sleeping: families slept together at one end of their houses, in their day-clothes. Series of niches arranged symmetrically in the walls served as shelves and cupboards. Stone pegs, placed between niches on a level with the lintels, made hooks for all purposes (*72*) and spare food and clothing was also stored in large jars. This was usually the extent of household furniture. Occasionally, as in the Ingenuity Group at Machu Picchu, one house had two boulders projecting through the floor; these were ingeniously carved into mortars in which maize could be ground and potatoes mashed. Simple stoves were constructed inside the house at the opposite end to that used for sleeping, but some were built against the outside wall in a corner of the compound. Very occasionally a small additional room was built beside a house with an outside entrance. This may have been used as a kitchen, but this theory still needs to be properly checked with excavations.

It has already been mentioned that inspectors were concerned with the level of hygiene in homes; this was not unproved by the Andean practice of sleeping on floors that consisted simply of beaten or well-trodden earth. The floors of some important structures were sometimes paved; small pebbles were used to pave the floor of the Coricancha temple in Cuzco. When a structure had a second-storey or an attic-storey, the floor was of wood, supported by recessing the walls. Access to this second storey was by a rope or rope ladder through the gable window and in rare instances stones have been found projecting from the outside corners of gable windows. Although some buildings with three storeys have been encountered, these were rare.

PALACES

Palaces were constructed along similar lines, whether they were built for the Emperor, his administrators, or for royal lodgings

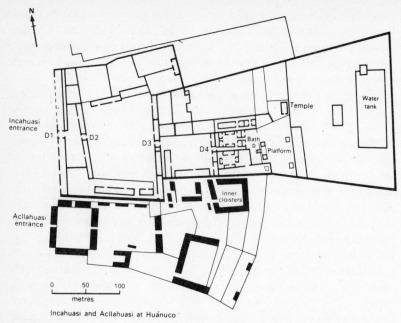

Incahuasi and Acllahuasi at Huánuco

52 *Plan of the Inca's palace at Huánuco, with the Acclahuasi shown beside it*
(After Harth-Terre)

and country or recreation houses. The principal royal palaces were spread over large sites and consisted of spacious single-roomed apartments, the only access to which was through the court onto which they opened (52). Murua gives the only illuminating descriptions of an Emperor's palace in Cuzco:

This great palace has two principal doorways, one at the main entrance and the other further inside from where one sees the magnificence of its workmanship better. At the entrance of the first doorway there were 2,000 indian soldiers, on guard, with their captain. . . . . At the second doorway was the armoury and arrows of the royal palace of the Inca, and . . . 100 captains, well-experienced in battle; further on there was another large court or patio for the palace officials and servants, and still further, there were the rooms and living rooms where the Inca lived. This was full of delights, because there were many kinds of trees and gardens, and the dwellings were very spacious and worked and adorned with much gold and carved engravings of the figures and exploits of the Inca's ancestors . . . at intervals there were niches and windows worked with silver and inset with precious stones.

In the palaces there were apartments for servants and attendants, and large reception halls which could hold up to 3,000 people under a single roof. Each palace had its own bathing suite, with large gold or silver basins and sometimes a sunken fitted-masonry bath; water flowed along fitted stone channels, hot water when hot springs were accessible. Smaller, more compact country palaces were built by the rulers in pleasant surroundings, away from the main towns. They were occupied periodically by the Emperor and were evidently intended primarily for relaxation and contemplation during the ruler's lifetime. However extensive terraces and agricultural lands were usually associated with this type, suggesting an investment for the support of the family descendants of the Sapa Inca's panaca. Royal lodgings, consisting of a compact walled enclosure with finely built structures arranged around a court, were also built beside the roads, for the Emperor to stay in when he travelled.

The palaces of important administrators varied only in size and prestige from those of the Emperor. Curacas of importance may have occupied palaces built in the Inca style, but many native leaders who lived in smaller settlements followed local building traditions. In the Colla and Chanca areas, round buildings continued to be built during the Inca period, and on the coast local materials and architectural forms (54) were widespread, indicating limited Inca influence.

53 Detail of the inner part of the Incahuasi, Huánuco

54 *View of a coastal Curaca's palace in the Rimac valley, reconstructed by Dr. Jiminex Borja*

The *Yachahuasi* schools for nobles were almost certainly constructed along similar lines to other palace compounds, but the *Acllahuasi* converts may have had some additional characteristic features; these were usually located near the Sun temples and accommodated at least 200 girls. The buildings had no windows opening onto the street, very high walls and a single guarded entrance. Men were forbidden to enter the Acllahuasi on pain of death. The following description by Garcilaso is based on those of his female relatives, who had access to the buildings:

> Amongst other notable features of this building there was a narrow passage wide enough for two persons, that ran the whole length of the building. The passage had many cells on either side of it, which were offices where women worked. At each door were trusted porters, and in the last apartment at the end of the passage, where no-one entered were the women of the Sun. . . .

Murúa infers that six different ranks of Chosen Women (Virgins), lived in six different structures. He goes on to say 'In the dwellings there were many rich hangings . . . cool gardens with trees . . . flowers . . . terraces . . . (and) water.' In the courtyards of the Acllahuasi the women spun and wove the finest clothing; they were also responsible for making chicha for the Sun and serving in the temple. Their living quarters were probably similar to the royal palaces, but remained more enclosed (52; ch 9, 90).

TEMPLES AND SHRINES

The main temples were constructed on prominent sites, often following a similar plan to that of the house or palace compound, although the shrines were not expected to shelter congregations. The Sun temple in Cuzco, the *Coricancha*, consisting of four small sanctuaries and a principal building, constructed of the finest fitted masonry, occupied and opened onto three sides of a court-yard. The smaller structures were arranged in two pairs on opposite sides of the court. The shrines were richly adorned, with plates of gold and silver covering the walls. Large and small niches were used as shelves for important cult objects; sometimes the large niches would contain the mummies of past rulers. A gold band, about a palm's width, was reported to have been set into masonry encircling the main temple like a cornice. The roofs were evidently of the 'hip' type and were elaborately ornamented with designs cut and woven into the ichu thatch with threads of gold, included to catch the light of the Sun. Many precious stones were set around the seats on which the Emperor and the Coya sat during important ceremonies.

Close by the Coricancha, there were many small dwellings built for the indian attendants who served the temple; in Cuzco we are told these attendants numbered 4,000. Also near the temple, was the *Intipampa* (Field of the Sun), an enclosure for sacrificial animals and a garden to the Sun. In this garden, according to Cieza, pieces of gold were scattered in imitation of clods of earth, golden maize was depicted with cobs of gold and leaves and stems of silver, and 20 llamas with a young life-sized shepherd were portrayed, all in gold.

Most of the chroniclers suggest that the temples built for the Sun throughout the empire were designed on the basis of the Cori-cancha prototype, although none of them give adequate descrip-tion of these to support the assumption. Fieldwork done suggests that, while many Sun temples show similarities to the Coricancha (55), this likeness varies according to the distance from Cuzco, and the influence of local climates and materials. For instance, at

55 *The temple site of Intihuatana, Pisac, is very similar in type and construction to that of Coricancha, Cuzco*

Pachacamac the Sun temple was built on the uppermost of several platforms, on an impressive pyramid. Building materials were also mainly local ones—adobes and stucco, covered with painted decoration. The buildings on top of the pyramid, however, provided ample accommodation for all the facilities in Coricancha, and included the main characteristics of the Inca style, such as trapezoidal niches.

Another type of temple consisted of a large single-roomed structure. It is not clear to which deity this was dedicated, perhaps in some cases to Viracocha, the Creator, and in others to the Sun. One example at Cacha, with internal supports and several storeys, was dedicated to Viracocha.

Inca shrines in the region of Cuzco include an open-air type distinguished by carvings in rocks, and associated directly or indirectly with formal construction (*70*). For instance at Kkenko, near the capital, a large upright natural rock, with a masonry platform, has a fine masonry semi-circular wall with niches on one of its sides. One tradition has it that the mummy of Pachacuti

Inca was kept in the rock mass, connected to the semi-circular platform. Cave shrines, cunningly sculpted and lined with masonry and niches, have also been found: beneath the peak of Huayna Picchu, two large caves were carved in this manner, and fine masonry rooms were built inside them (*89*); outside the caves, there were quarters for a priest and storage.

GARDENS

Since gardens occupied such a decorative and important place in the architecture of Sun temples and palaces, to Cieza's account of the Sun temple's gardens (p. 131) should be added Garcilaso's description of an Inca's palace gardens. The gardens were usually set in the shape of a courtyard, or on terraces:

> Here were planted the finest trees and most beautiful flowers and sweet smelling herbs in the kingdom, while quantities of others were reproduced in gold and silver, at every stage of their growth from the sprout that hardly shows above the earth, to the full-blown plant, in complete maturity. There were also fields of corn with silver stalks and golden ears, on which the leaves, grains, and even the corn silk were shown. In addition to all this there were all kinds of gold and silver animals in these gardens, such as rabbits, mice, lizards, snakes, butterflies, foxes and wild-cats; there were birds set in the trees and others bent over the flowers, breathing in their nectar. There were roedeer, and deer, pumas and jaguars and all animals in creation, each placed just where it should be.

PRISONS

Prison buildings were probably rare, since offenders were usually punished immediately, and the prisons may have functioned primarily as places of execution and corporal punishment. Guaman Poma deals with this subject at some length—indeed one suspects him of particular interest and even of relish. In addition, his drawings of the subject are particularly lucid (*30*). He records three main types of prisons.

'*Uatay Uaci Zancay* (the subterranean prison) . . for big crimes. . . . It was constructed under the ground, in the form of a cave, it was very dark, and here they kept vipers and poisonous serpents, pumas, . . . animals that served the punishment.' Traitors, thieves, witches and those who insulted the Emperor were punished here. This type of prison existed only in the cities, since it had to be 'supported'. (Elsewhere this type of prison is referred to as the

56 Many small and round and square storehouses line hillsides near provincial capitals

Samca-huasi, meaning the 'House of Horror'.)

Arauay and *Uimpillay*, near Cuzco, were places of execution where thieves and adulterers were executed or punished. Arauay was 'the place where women were tied by their hair' (*30*).

In the third category, second-class prisons had facilities for retaining persons awaiting trial—also, facilities for torturing them; first-class prisons were for important curacas and prisoners holding some social position of prestige, who were held in an enclosed compound with houses where they could be visited. While these may have been unique to Cuzco, the others were probably found in provincial capitals.

57 Large rectangular storehouses of two storeys are located in small groups on the Cuzco area, as at Pisac

STOREHOUSES

Most storehouses were built in regular rows along hillsides, near the larger towns. There were sometimes as many as 500 outside provincial capitals (as at Huánuco) constructed to house supplies of all kinds: food, clothes, army stores, weapons, tools. Their location was high to avoid damp, and the two or three metres (6.5 or 9 ft) which separated them reduced the danger of spreading fires. In cool areas the buildings were quite small, round or square to rectangular forms, without niches (56). In some cases there was only a window for removing the contents, and access was gained by projecting stone steps up the surface of the wall.

Another type of storehouses were large, two-storeyed rectangular structures, built in the Urubamba valley and sometimes on the sides of valleys in the Cuzco region. These occur in isolation or in small groups and their many full-length windows provided additional ventilation (57).

FORTRESSES

The diversity of the fortress plans demonstrates the individual creativity of the Inca engineers and architects in solving problems. Each fortress was planned to its specific topographical setting, which was carefully selected for maximum efficiency.

Most fortresses were basically citadel fortresses incorporating a variety of facilities, which enabled refugees and defenders to survive for considerable periods of time when under attack or without supply lines. However, they were built for many reasons: citadels were built outside, but close to, towns as at Cajamarca, Cusichaca (59) and in the case of Sacsahuaman at Cuzco (39); some citadel fortresses were built specifically to facilitate conquest and to control subject populations, as at Paramonga (37) and in Bolivia and Chile. The citadel town—which by its topographical situation was quite naturally defended—like that of Machu Picchu (*frontispiece*), may have been planned in this form because of the topographical characteristics of the area, where adequate low-lying sites were not available.

The citadel fortresses provided for accommodation, as well as a water supply and storage. Defensive terracing, series of great zig-zagging fortifications, strategic towers and observation posts, (58) occur on those sides which were more susceptible to attack, while natural impassable slopes provided adequate protection on the remaining sides.

58 Lookouts at Pisac; their outer walls follow the curving contours of the terrain

59 The residential fort of Huillca Raccay in the foreground controlled the flow of traffic up and down the valley. Opposite lies the administrative centre of Patallacta

TOMBS

No tombs of the Inca nobles have been found intact in the Cuzco region, so that it is impossible to be sure of what these consisted; certain finely carved chambers in natural rock masses are often associated with local stories and legends, which identify them as the tombs of important Incas. There exists, however, little direct archaeological evidence to support this interpretation.

Numerous ordinary tombs are known and these vary, depending partly on their location. Many small beehive tombs, usually of field-stones laid in clay, were built against cliffs and in large rock shelters or under overhanging boulders, which gave them protection from rainfall (60). Many of these tombs were also free-standing, round or square in shape, with corbel-vaulted roofs, and sometimes, a coating of mud stucco. Such tombs were called *chullpas*. Both size and shape varied, but each had a small door which was blocked after the body had been placed in a flexed seated position inside. Some tombs were family burial places.

Poma draws pictures of the different types of burial practices of the Andeans: the Chinchaysuyus were buried in a small corbelled, domed chullpa; the Antisuyus placed their dead in a hollowed tree trunk; the Collasuyus had fine burials in large chullpas; the Cuntisuyus seem to have followed the practice of the Collasuyus, although in the coastal regions burials were usually under the ground.

COMMUNICATIONS

Observation posts, tollgates and Chasqui posts were regularly encountered along the Inca roads. Small structures, built beside the road in positions of maximum visibility, were occupied by officials responsible for control of traffic of persons and goods. Since trade was a government monopoly, toll-gates did not levy taxes but only checked or counted the goods.

At the Chasqui posts, two runners occupied each of two small stone huts. Built of fieldstones, the form varying slightly in each province, these posts were built at about two-kilometre (1-mile) intervals. One man slept while the other runner waited to take relayed messages or quipus containing information on to the next post. The average speed of the runners, who ran as fast as they could, was approximately four times faster than a horseman could travel over the roads. Beacon fires were used for more urgent

60 Tombs located in crevices along the cliff-face at Pisac

messages. The roads, tambos, and Chasqui posts were serviced by the provinces in which they were located. The runners were trained from boyhood and were severely punished if a message miscarried. Poma suggests that the runners were the sons of the curacas and other officials.

The Incas built over 25,000 kilometres (15,500 miles) of all-weather roads for men and llama caravans, from sea level to a height of about 5,500 metres (17,500 ft). The two main royal roads ran parallel to each other: one through the Andes, which passed over sierras and plateaux buried in snow, through deep valleys and damp forests; the other along the coast, through barren desert and over wide river mouths. The royal roads, cut by important secondary networks, connected all the major towns and provinces. Distance markers called *topo* were placed along some roads and measured distances of just over 10 kilometres (6 miles).

The highland road ran over extremes of topography and climatic conditions where the invention of the wheel, in the bronze age, would have been of little use. Also, had there been larger beasts of burden they would certainly have slipped and fallen with their loads in places where the roads had to be stepped, or narrow channels cut through solid rock. Stone terraced and paved roads were constructed on hillsides and precipitous mountainsides, sometimes passing along the steep sides of a sheer rock face, where walls were placed in dangerous places and corners. Fierce mountain rivers were crossed by reed-plaited suspension bridges, hundreds of feet long, anchored on a pair of stone towers at each end, or by a basket cable car where there was less traffic. Streams were crossed by wooden or corbelled stone bridges, and anyone who destroyed or burnt a bridge, without orders to do so, was 'executed with vigour'. In the highlands the road measurements varied between a width of 1.50 metres (5 ft), in difficult terrain where it was zig-zagged or stepped, and a maximum width of about 6 metres (19.5 ft) along wide terraces on lower valley sides, where an even contour could be maintained. The road was stone-laid in muddy country, and fashioned into wide stone-paved causeways with culverts for drainage when crossing bogs.

The coastal road was consistently wide (about 5 metres, or 16.5 ft, in width) and straight, but was not surfaced. Along its sides were sand-guarding walls of stone or adobes, about a metre (3.33 ft) high, which also guided, and facilitated the control of, armies and llamas. In the valleys these were even painted, and were accompanied by water-channels, but in barren areas the road was sometimes marked only by posts at intervals, so that no one should lose their way. Floating pontoon bridges, consisting of a row of *balsas* (reed boats) were tethered and a road bed of wood was constructed to permit passage over wide rivers.

7

Country life

AGRICULTURE

Under the Incas there were two main systems of agriculture: the highland staple root crops which had been domesticated locally over thousands of years to altitudes up to 5,000 metres (about 16,500 ft); and maize, the warm-weather crop grown on the lower slopes and protected valley-floors of the highlands and the lowlands. Murra (see Bibliography) considers that Andean agricultural ritual in the highlands reveals significant differences between two ways of life, based on these two systems of agriculture, and that one of these, the wider cultivation of maize under the Incas, was in the process of incorporating and transforming the other, when this development was interrupted by the Spanish invasion.

In the high altitudes, frost-resistant tubers and herding went together. Of the tubers, the potato is the best known and has been found blooming at 5,000 metres (16,500 ft) in 18 degrees of frost. The importance of the potato can best be illustrated by the fact that time was measured in units equivalent to the time it took to boil a potato! Until quite recently 220 varieties were still grown in the Collao. In the highest altitude, the slow-ripening and bitter varieties were grown for chuño, which could be kept for 'many years' according to Cobo. This process (p. 40) is dependent on cold nights, warm days and a dry climate; where these conditions were lacking the Andeans could not store the root crops effectively. Maize, on the other hand, while it is easily stored for longer periods than chuño, is a handicapped crop in the highlands since it is killed by frost.

There are other basic differences between potatoes and maize. Maize requires steady watering and fertilizing, but if grown in these conditions, it is not necessary for the land to lie fallow, nor for crops to be rotated; potatoes, on the other hand, can be grown in normal conditions of rainfall without irrigation or fertilizers, but the land must be left fallow after four years of cultivation, for seven years.

The Incas were able greatly to extend the cultivation of maize in the highlands, under their socio-economic organization, as a 'state crop'. In pre-*Inca* times in most highland areas, maize was grown (or acquired through exchange), mainly for ceremonial purposes. Under the Incas, it was also grown primarily as a high-status food—for beer-making and ceremonial purposes—but it was much more generally grown, and was available from the storehouses throughout the empire. In fact, Murra has suggested that 'a major function [of the mitimaes] was actually the expansion of the maize growing area'. This policy often coincided with that of settlement for security reasons, and could have been a factor in all three types of mitima resettlement programmes.

Coca, a low bush whose leaves release cocaine when chewed in a wad with lime, was grown in the wet Andean lowlands of the montaña, east of Cuzco. Coca was used as a stimulant, mainly in connection with religious ritual, by the priesthood and the élite. Although it had the effect of calming sensations of hunger, thirst and tiredness, the Incas limited its use and carefully supervised the distribution of the leaves. Highland indians suffered great discomfort and rapidly fell prey to disease in the montaña; the Incas therefore cultivated only a limited supply of these leaves, using lowland mit'a workers and criminals sent there for punishment from the highlands. Members of the élite carried coca leaves in small bags, and the leaf was offered in sacrifices. It was during the Spanish colonial period that this leaf was intensively cultivated and sold to the indians throughout the Andean area.

Fertilizers used in the Andean area varied. On the coast droppings of the guano birds, very rich in nitrogen, were collected and distributed on the land. The Incas also transported guano, sardine and small fishes heads, also used on the coast, into the highlands for use on maize fields. The only fertilizers available locally to the highlanders were llama dung in the higher regions and human excreta in the lower valleys.

The *Inca* are credited with inventing the *taclla* foot-plough. Both this plough and the *qorana*, a hoe, the two most important farming implements, had their efficiency increased by the use of bronze. The foot-plough (*63*) consisted of a pole about 1.8 metres

(6ft) long, with a hardened wood or bronze digging point, a foot-rest near the point, and a handle on the holding end. It was used for breaking up the ground, digging holes and harvesting potatoes. The hoe, lighter to handle, was used more for general cultivation, breaking up clods and weeding; its short shaft had a wide, chisel-shaped, bronze blade. In addition to these implements, a clod-breaker was used to break up loosened earth, and a boat-shaped board for scraping earth over planted seeds (63).

Well-organized and dependable agricultural surpluses, that could be easily kept and stored, were essential to the Inca sociopolitical structure. The well-irrigated coastal valleys probably supplied one of the most reliable yearly quotas to the Incas' storehouses. Other important areas, prominent in maize production, were the larger, warmer valleys, such as the Urubamba, Tarma and Cochabamba.

TERRACING AND IRRIGATION WORKS

Agricultural terraces were built in the Andes to prevent erosion of the hillsides, and to extend the area of level land available for cultivation. Although the pre-*Inca* peoples built some terraces, these were small and fragmented undertakings while those built by the Incas surpassed all others, being much superior in construction. The latter were huge engineeering undertakings, carefully built of stone in extensive series along the valley sides. On steep slopes terraces were narrow, perhaps only 1.50 metres (5ft) wide, but lower down, where the terraces became wider, they sometimes attained an area equivalent to a small farm at the bottom of a slope.

The mit'a was brought in to construct the terraces according to plans laid out by the engineers. First, a terrace wall was built, slightly inclined to better hold the infill; the base of the terrace was then partly filled with rubble, on top of which fertile alluvial soil, brought from the valley floor, was deposited (61). Long banks of terraces curved to the contours of a hillside or followed straighter-line formations along the valley floor, sometimes beside a canalized river. Access to the different terraces was gained by small stone stairways, which also acted as drainage channels permitting surface water from upper slopes to flow freely down. Other terraces had projecting stepping stones in their inclined walls with stone-channels carved in masonry blocks to effect water drainage.

61 The Urubamba river was canalized and the valley sides terrained

Irrigation works constructed by the Incas, brought water over long distances, maintaining an efficient agricultural economy, on which the empire depended. Masonry channels, about 60 centimetres (24 in.) wide, were built of carefully laid stones in mud mortar, usually along gentle contoured slopes, but sometimes stepped on very steep gradients, where the water cascaded in descent like a small waterfall. Single masonry blocks, laid end to end, were used primarily in and near towns. In the town they were often covered and ran underground. These carved, fitted blocks were also used to carry water down the terraces and to fountains. Ditches were widely employed on flatter ground, and were supported by terraces along low gradient hillsides where a gentle contour could be maintained.

Aqueducts were sometimes used to cross a valley or maintain a gradient. At Tipon, in the Cuzco valley, a stone aqueduct was built with tapering walls (*62*, it still supports its narrow fitted masonry channel). Nearby, a fine stone-lined reservoir tank, measuring approximately 30 by 20 metres (32 by 22 yds.), collects water which is then distributed over a series of terraces and is deposited in some fountain baths and at an Inca 'country residence'. Another method used for carrying water across narrower terrain, or over a narrow river gorge—as in one unique instance to Patallacta (at Cusichaca)—was to utilize a hollowed-out tree trunk.

Some highland rivers were canalized by the Incas, to prevent damage to precious land where the river continually changed course, washing away the good alluvial soil. For this reason the Urubamba was largely canalized and was straightened at Pisac and Ollantaytambo. This canal survives today, but the banks are in danger of giving way, due to the accumulation of deposits (61). At Cusichaca, a site located half-way between Machu Picchu and Ollantaytambo, the extensive landscape planning of the Incas can be fully appreciated (59): a small river entering the Urubamba was canalized in a straight line through a valley and then in a broad curve, passed around an alluvial fan, with petal-shaped agricultural terraces, which reached the terraced river bank. Above the terraces, the town of Patallacta was supported on a further series of narrow semicircular terraces.

62 An aqueduct and a reservoir at Tipon, Cuzco valley

LAND TENURE AND TAX

Land belonged to kin groups (the panaca or ayllu), rather than to individuals. At the top of the hierarchy, the produce from the land owned by a ruler's panaca (his descendants) was shared by all his sons present at the sowing of the crops. Similarly, those men who had received tax-free gifts of land from the Emperor, received them for themselves and their descendants. Such lands might be given as rewards for battle deeds, bridge-building, irrigation schemes and inventions. They were also sometimes given to very favoured sons of curacas who had served well. A condition was that this land could not be exchanged (sold), or transferred, divided or disposed of in any way. The chief member of the ayllu divided it each year between the kin, so that all the sons should have equal parts in proportion to their dependants, and all had to share in the working of the land (or at least attend at the sowing ceremony). When an absentee returned, so did his rights. Cobo tells us that, even when there were so many members of an ayllu sharing this 'private' land that each received only one maize cob, the custom still had to be maintained.

The rest of the lands in the empire were divided (p. 58) between the Inca Emperor, the Sun and other cults, and the community. These divisions were not necessarily equal in size and varied in different parts. They were made locally according to the area of land under cultivation and the population to be supported.

In the lands of the Emperor and the Religion (p. 58), overseers and administrators were placed to organize cultivation and harvesting, while the work of sowing and harvesting was the tax contribution of the male householders.

The boundaries of the lands were carefully measured and maintained with markers. A measuring stick based on the *rikra* (a fathom measuring 162 cm., or 65 in.), was kept for checking land measurements when boundaries were disputed. In some accounts land measurements are also referred to as *topo*, but its size is uncertain (see Rowe 1946), probably comprising of one or two acres or an area of land which varied according to the size of the family it supported. Anyone who moved the boundary stones or markers, or entered foreign hereditary land, was punished. A heavy stone was dropped on his shoulders for a first offence, and the death penalty was received for a second.

The lands of the Emperor and Religion were treated with considerable reverence by the Andeans: no one dared to cross these fields without reverent phrases especially conjured for this purpose. There were special laws concerning their cultivation, and anyone who casually stole produce to eat as he walked beside them was executed. On the other hand, if he took food from another commoner's land he was pardoned.

The lands dedicated to Religion were divided between the Sun, Thunderbolt, and the other deities and idols of local belief. Each was given land in proportion to the importance of its cult and, thus, to the number of priests and attendants in its service, who had to be supported. The working and protection of these lands was considered one of the most important religious duties of the people. When it was time to sow or cultivate the lands, all other tasks were stopped so that all taxpayers could take part— with the exception of those who were on urgent government business, or were fighting a war. Everyone assembled to cultivate the lands of the Religion before the other lands, inaugurating the season's work with ceremonials in the presence of important dignitaries: the most important man present—and this applied even to the Emperor himself—started the sowing work with a golden *taclla* (plough or digging stick, *63*). Then all the other important persons and nobles present followed his example, their wives kneeling facing the men to break the clods. However, the nobles soon stopped working, in the order that they had begun, and sat down to a festival and banquets, while the Curaca Pachaca worked a little longer and then supervised the commoners who remained at the task.

The common householders and their foremen worked all day, dividing by lines the area they were each responsible for. Each man put his family to work on his section: he who had most helpers finished his part first and was considered a rich man. Once the lands of Religion were finished, everyone again assembled, and the same ceremonies were repeated as the sowing was started on the Emperor's lands. As they sowed the Religion's lands, the workers sang appropriate rythmic songs in praise of the deities, and when they cultivated the Emperor's lands, in his praise.

Last to be cultivated were the community lands. These, it was understood, were the Emperor's lands for the public use, but in practice they belonged to the community. In each community sufficient lands were retained for the population. The curacas divided them each year between the householders in proportion to the size of their families, additional amounts being added for each child. Some land was left to fallow—and it has been suggested that it was partly to enforce a proper rotation of crops that the yearly distribution was made. If a taxpayer was absent for some acceptable reason, the other members of the community worked his fields in exchange only for their day's food ration. After working the lands of absentees, they cultivated their own fields.

The curacas were responsible also for organizing the distribution of water, needed to irrigate the lands. Anyone who opened the sluice gates and 'stole' water with which the land was to be irrigated, or took it before his turn, was punished.

After harvesting time, produce from the lands was kept in government storehouses and granaries built for Religion and the Inca Emperor. One group of storehouses into which crops were placed by the community indians, was situated on the land from which the produce had been gathered. The produce was then taken to storehouses situated outside the provincial capitals, where those of the Emperor were the more numerous, indicating that his lands were also somewhat more extensive than those of the Religion. At the end of the year, some part of this produce (depending on the quantity of the harvest), was then taken to Cuzco for the Capac Raymi festival. The produce of Religion was transported to Cuzco on the llamas owned by Religion, and accompanied by men who ate at the expense of Religion. Similarly the Emperor's produce was brought on the backs of his animals and he provided for those who accompanied it. Not all areas had large herds of llamas, and from areas such as Ecuador, where they were particularly scarce, the produce was transported on the backs of men, who could in fact carry heavier loads than the llamas. In the latter case the men were fed at the owner's expense.

In the provinces, part of the provisions in the Emperor's storehouses, when they were not otherwise needed, were distributed to the people, especially in times of hardship, and, on a more regular basis, to the poor. Exchanges of goods between regions were also made in the redistribution of this produce which was moved around by the government as it was needed. The organization of traffic and goods was extremely efficiently looked after by overseers and accountants, so that no place ran out of stores, and the lodges and tambos were always full of supplies for travellers.

AGRICULTURAL RITUAL

In the chronicles, the Inca ceremonial calendar cycle is described

63 Ritual maize sowing in August, followed by more general sowing in September

as dealing largely with agriculture, notably with maize, but more recent studies have suggested that there were also elaborate ceremonies to protect and encourage potato crops. In the cultivation of both maize and root crops, but specifically maize, many ceremonies, including fasting and sacrifices, were employed to persuade the forces of nature to provide the best conditions for a successful harvest.

The importance given to maize by the Incas is well illustrated in an origin myth which refers to 'the seed of the cave' (cave of origin) and to the introduction of maize into the Cuzco basin by their ancestors. Maize was the colour of the Sun's rays and was given a privileged position in the Coricancha's garden, Intipampa (Field of the Sun). Every year the priests performed the ritual of asking the gods if maize crops should be planted: of course, they always received an affirmative answer. They then watched the movements of the shadow on certain 'sundials' placed near Cuzco, which were towers constructed in order to ascertain the equinoxes (p. 200). From these towers the priests could read the right time for ploughing, irrigation, and planting, in order to advise the agricultural workers all over the empire, thus ensuring a good crop. Prayers, followed by offerings, were made by local farmers to further ensure the safety of their crops: 'O fountain of water which for so many years has watered my field, through which blessing I gather my food, do thou the same this year and even give more water, that the harvest may be more abundant.'

The Andeans were also alert for omens by which they could estimate their harvest. Processions were organized to scare away

64 Working in the maize fields; weeding in January, and protecting crops from pests in February and March

drought, frost or birds, during which gongs were beaten; young children were given the task of watching the fields and using their slings should birds or other animals disturb the ripening corn. The year's harvest, like the sowing, was officially and ceremoniously begun in Cuzco by the royal candidates for Huarachico, who reaped a terrace dedicated to Mama Huaco (a sister-wife of Manco Capac), the patroness of maize. The harvests were accompanied by sacrifices, thanksgiving offerings, and much dancing, feasting and chicha drinking. In every house a shrine was created for 'mother maize' by wrapping the best cobs in the family's finest cloth.

The Inca agricultural cycle as depicted by Poma is shown in figures 63, 64, 65. The calendar began, in the highlands, with a lunar month corresponding to parts of August and September when the inauguration of the agricultural year was marked by the maize sowing ritual. Early potatoes and maize were planted along with the slower-ripening varieties. At the September equinox young maize shoots began to appear: birds and animal pests were kept away from the crops by boys with slings, the other dangers being frosts and drought. In November the maize fields needed irrigation and small ditches were dug to distribute the water from main sources and reservoirs evenly over the fields. In December coca was planted, without the use of irrigation. In January, the month of the most rainfall, the growing plants were weeded and hilled (banked up with soil). Although early potatoes could be harvested in January, most root crops were harvested in February and March. During these months, the maize crop was

65 Harvesting the maize in May; the potatoes in June

already high and was guarded day and night by the young people. The maize began to ripen in April and human thieves, according to Poma, had to be discouraged, as well as birds and animals like foxes, deer and skunk. The maize crop was finally ready to be harvested in May (*Amoray* month): the maize was kept dry, husked and deposited in storehouses, the best grains for food and the poorest for beer. In June, the large potatoes were dug up and the early ones planted to produce a third crop and in July the potatoes and crops were stored and irrigation ditches were cleaned.

The importance of maize is also illustrated by its role in family life, even in villages where it was not grown: maize and llamas were among the gifts offered at Rutuchico, Huarachico, and also at marriage. Maize flour was, in addition, used in many healing 'cures' cleansing rituals, and was sprinkled around the deceased.

Although few rituals connected with the cultivation of potatoes were recorded by the early chroniclers, one was described in considerable detail by Cieza. The account was obtained in 1547 from a Spanish priest in whose diocese of Lampa-lampa in the Titicaca region it took place:

I, Marcos Otazo, resident of Valladolid, being in the village of Lampaz instructing the indians in our Christian faith, in the year of 1547, the month of May, in the full of the moon, there came to me all the caciques (*curaca*) and headmen to beg me most earnestly to give them permission to do what they were in the habit of doing at that season. I replied that I would have to be present, for if it was something not licit for our Holy Catholic faith, they were not to do it henceforth. They agreed to this, and they all went to their homes.

And when it was, as I could judge, exactly noon, from different directions came the sound of the beating of many drums, played with a single stick, for that is their way of playing them, and then blankets were spread on the ground in the square, like carpets, for the caciques and headmen to sit on, all decked out and dressed in their best clothes, their hair hanging in a four-strand braid on each side, as is their custom. When they were seated, I saw a boy of about 12 advance toward each of the caciques; he was the handsomest and most agile of all, and richly dressed after their fashion, with his legs from the knee down covered with red tassels, and his arms the same, and on his body he wore many medals and ornaments of gold and silver. In his right hand he carried a kind of arm like a halberd, and in his left, a bag of wool in which they carry coca. ..

On his left side came a girl of about ten, very pretty, dressed in the same fashion, except that she wore a long shirt, which the other women are not in the habit of wearing , and this (a train) was carried by an older indian woman, very handsome and with an air of authority. Behind her came many other indian women, like ladies-in-waiting, with great poise and breeding. And that girl carried in her right hand a beautiful woollen bag, covered with ornaments of gold and silver, and from her shoulders hung a small puma skin which completely covered her back. Behind these women there followed six indians representing farmers, each with his plough on his shoulder, and on their head diadems and feathers, very beautiful and of many colours. These were followed by six more, like helpers, with bags of potatoes, playing the drum, and in order they came to within a step of the cacique.

The boys and girls I have described, and all the rest in turn, made him a deep bow, lowering their heads, and the cacique and headmen bowed in return. When this had been done to each cacique, for there were two of them, in the same order in which they had come the boy and others moved backward without turning their faces, some 20 paces, in the order I have described. There the farmers sank their ploughs in the ground in a row, and hung from them those bags of potatoes, large and carefully selected; and when they had done this, playing their drums, they began a kind of dance without moving from where they were standing, on the tips of their toes, and from time to time they lifted the bags they had in their hands towards the sky. Only those I have mentioned did this, those who accompanied this boy and girl, and all the ladies-in-waiting; for the caciques and other people, seated in order of rank, watched and listened in silence.

When this was finished they sat down, and a yearling llama was brought in, uniform in colour, without a single blemish, by other indians who had gone for it. In front of the cacique, surrounded by so many other indians I could not see it, they stretched it out on the ground, and, still alive, removed all its entrails through one side, and gave them to the soothsayers, whom they call *huaca-camayocs*, who are the priests among us. And I observed that certain of the indians quickly scooped up as much of the llama's blood as they could in their hands, and sprinkled it over the potatoes in the bags. At that moment a headman, who had turned Christian a few days before, as I shall tell, rushed forward shouting and calling them dogs and . . . upbraided them for that diabolical rite . . . they went away frightened and confused, without concluding their sacrifice by which they foretell the crops and events of the entire year.

This ritual for sowing potatoes was no doubt closely related to traditional Colla customs, but it was probably also incorporated into Inca ritual practices.

HERDING

Herding and root staples went together in the Andean economy. The cameloids—the llama, the alpaca, vicuña and guanaco— had their different uses, while the llama had a long history of domestication (p. 22). The grasslands of the high slopes and plateaux were concentrated in southern Peru and Bolivia, where the llama is believed to have first been domesticated, due to the high local concentration of both wild and domesticated species. The chroniclers described the llama as 'a friend of cold climates' where it ate the fodder growing among the ichu grass, and evidently the animal suffered in the hot coastal lands and climates, to which it was sent only to carry supplies and as meat, to supplement the coastal diet. Few llamas and alpacas were found in Ecuador: they were probably introduced to the area by the Inca distribution policy, shortly before the Spanish invasion. The guanaco and vicuña had a wider habitat and roamed wild in many areas.

The llama was the only animal in the Andean area large enough to be used as a pack animal (66). It could travel about 20 kilometres (12 miles) a day with a load of up to 45 kg. (100 lb.); docile when comfortable, if overloaded the animal would lie down and refuse to budge. Its wool was coarse but could be used to make cloth-like sacks and plaited ropes. The alpacas, smaller animals with finer, softer wool, were shorn regularly and were kept

66 Loaded llama

primarily for their fleece. But it was the wild vicuña that provided the most luxurious silk-like wool, the consistency of which was highly regarded by the Inca élite. These animals were caught and fleeced in the annuals or seasonal hunts. As mentioned before, all cameloids provided meat, which was preserved as charqui, and leather, as well as other commodities such as manure for burning, or fertilizer.

The Colla, who lived in the heartland of the llama homeland, were the most important llama and alpaca breeders. In this area the 3,242 householders of Juli reported a community herd of 16,846 head in 1567, while larger herds were evidently maintained in the Inca period. Murra points out that there were two distinct aspects to Andean animal husbandry: that of the defeated ethnic groups and that of the Inca government.

Herding was traditionally thought of, as it is today, as a job for the young people of both sexes. However, during the Inca period large herds in important herding areas were assigned to full-time shepherds, whose rights of access to agricultural lands were maintained, their lands being worked for them by their kin. Some herders continued to work on a rotation basis while others became the pastoral retainers, maintained by the Inca government and Colla chiefs. These herders lived permanently in the *puna* grasslands with their wives and families, and expected 'gifts' of food, coca leaves, and beer, as well as full subsistence: they were the herders of religious and government flocks, and were entirely responsible for the animals, of which careful accounts had to be kept. They also carried out a number of supplementary tasks such as hunting deer and guanacos for meat; gathering feathers for the government weavers; and fishing. They and their families also made plaited ropes from the llama wool. In a successful year, in which the flocks increased, these men were rewarded with additional bonus supplies of food and clothing. When a herder died only one of his sons inherited the post while the rest returned to their community of origin.

The Incas maintained a similar division of pasture lands, as they did with agricultural lands, so that the tame herds of alpacas and llamas raised for the Religion, the Emperor, and the community were kept separate. Pastures of the Religion and the Emperor were called *moyas* (gardens). In a given province, each had its set boundary limits and different provinces could not share the same pastures, even for the herds of the same owner. The community herds in most regions, at least outside the Collao, were much smaller than those of the Religion or the Emperor. The animals belonging to the Religion were used mainly for sacrifices, although some formed herds which were attached to shrines, for their support, and some provided transport for the Religion's produce. The Emperor's animals were used as pack animals, for food, and for wool, which was distributed to everyone in the empire for their home use, and in addition, for *cumbi* cloth, woven by professional weavers and Mamacunas (Consecrated Women). Although the ordinary taxpayer was allowed only up to ten animals, nobles could acquire more as gifts from the Emperor. These privately owned animals were never taxed. Community herds usually contained all those animals owned by the local kin groups, whose animals were specially ear-marked or branded. Individual owners maintained rights over certain animals.

In Inca animal husbandry, two strict rules had to be observed: animals that contracted a fatal and contagious mange, called *caracha*, were to be immediately killed and buried, to prevent the disease from spreading; secondly no female animals were to be killed in sacrifices, or for any other reason, unless they caught caracha. The herders had their own special songs and ritual and they worshipped *Urcuchillay*, a vari-coloured buck who watched over the llamas growth and reproduction cycle (p. 189). The herders had warm clothes and compact huts in which to find shelter from the icy winds of the puna. They built dry-stone or sod corrals for the llamas.

Every year, hundreds of llamas carried wool, potatoes and

charqui from the puna lands to the coast—to be exchanged for maize, chili peppers and other coastal produce. They were driven by men who were supported by the Inca government. The goods for exchange were often grown by colonists and their descendants, so that barter played only a small part in these transactions. The herders, however, were permitted to do some bartering, and make some exchanges on their own account. Usually about eight drivers were used for every hundred animals.

HUNTING AND FISHING

The wild herds of guanacos, vicuñas and deer were deployed and organized in hunting grounds in each province, the people of one province not being allowed to hunt, or interfere with animals in another province. In fact, the hunting grounds all belonged to the Inca Emperor and no one could hunt in them without his permission or that of his governor. Such a licence was granted at certain seasons, or for limited quantities of meat or wool when there were shortages. It was always forbidden to kill the female animals. Vicuñas were captured alive in order to be shorn. Slings, bolas, snares, and nooses were used to capture the animals once they were driven into the centre of a circle of hunters.

A rectangular net attached to poles was used to catch birds (29), which were taken chiefly for their feathers but also for sacrifices. Animals that were considered pests such as foxes, pumas and bears were killed mainly by clubs, which were used on the animals when they were brought to bay. In one of the last imperial hunts, organized by Manco Inca in 1536, 10,000 indians formed a ring some 50–100 kilometres (30 to 60 miles) in circumference. When the circle closed, designated hunters killed over 11,000 animals, not counting those remaining which were freed. To surround vicuñas and guanacos another technique was sometimes used which forced them into a narrow gorge.

Fishing was less important around Cuzco, where there are few lakes and the rivers are too shallow and swift, than it was around Lake Titicaca. The *Uru*, considered a backward people by the Incas, lived almost entirely on the fish they caught from the waters of that lake. On becoming the subjects of the Incas, the latter benevolently permitted these lake-dwellers to pay their tribute in fish, granting them fishing rights in return.

The other important fishing area was, of course, that of the coast. The coastal fishermen used copper fishhooks and a two-man net, drawn up between boats. Fishermen here also made weirs along the beaches to catch the fish between tides. Techniques in the highlands may have included the use of large dip-nets, pronged fish-spears or dammed streams.

While in the Inca homeland there was little reason to make boats, these were important on large lakes, like Titicaca, and on the coast. Several kinds of craft were made from bundles of tortora reeds by the Aymara, to navigate the lakes and rivers. Based on more recent studies by Dr H. Tschopik Jr. a clearer picture of these craft can be obtained. Small, one-man *balsas* (reed boats) were made of four cigar-shaped bundles of the reeds, each approximately 2.4 to 3.7 metres (8 to 12 ft) in length, the two larger bundles forming the bottom of the craft. A pole, in the form of a fork-handled sculling oar, was used in shallow water from a standing position; in deep water it was operated like a paddle, from a kneeling or sitting position (*67*).

Large balsas, 4.5 to 6.1 metres (14 to 20 ft) in length, were equipped with a mast of two poles in the form of an inverted V, and a wooden hook at the top for raising and lowering the sail. In these sailing balsas, the fork-handled sculling oar was kept in an oarlock at the rear. The sail was used only in a following wind since the tacking method was probably unknown. Shelter was supplied by reed mats on a bent-pole frame. For anchoring the boats with their noses to the wind, large stones, perforated or grooved around the middle, were used.

Small fishing balsas made on the coast were similar to those made by the Aymara, except that they had long tapering prows and square-cut sterns; they were light enough to be carried by

67 Balsa boat used for fishing on Lake Titicaca

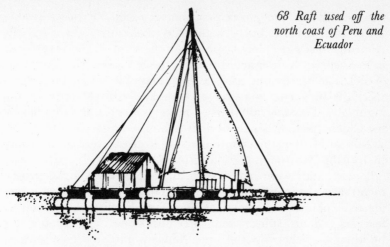

68 Raft used off the north coast of Peru and Ecuador

one man. Groups of these craft, each propelled by a man using a split-cane double-headed paddle had a range of about 28 kilometres (17½ miles) from the coastline. Another type of craft, made of inflated seal skins lashed together, supported one man and was very light. This type was reported from Arica and Tarapata, where the fishermen had to carry tubes through which they could blow into the skins.

Other craft included floats, made of many gourds put into a net and propelled by swimmers, and rough cane rafts, built as emergency ferries across rivers. Peruvian sea navigation was limited largely by the lack of convenient supplies of suitable timber. But along the coast of North Peru to Manta in Ecuador, large seagoing balsawood rafts were built from the local timber supply (*68*). It was one of these that Pizarro sighted off the South American coast during his reconnaissance voyage.

OTHER RURAL TASKS AND ACTIVITIES

Many of the other rural tasks, such as collecting firewood, were carried out by the young and by the older members of the community. In some areas, where it was plentiful, there was free wood for the taking; however, in the sparsely wooded areas the Emperor took possession, and the wood could only be cut and removed by permission. To prevent stripping, licence was granted according to individual needs. Fuel was a serious problem in many highland valleys and in the puna lands, where no trees can grow. Bushes and scrub were also precious, and were used sparingly for fuel;

however, llama dung was particularly useful for this purpose, since when dried it burns with little smoke or odour. That the Andeans were extremely fastidious in their use of wood is evident in their carefully designed stove, which used a very small amount of fuel. The ceremonial use of carved logs of wood for burning as sacrifices in Cuzco may have symbolized this scarcity in the highlands. This specially carved resinous wood was provided by the Chicha people as part of their tribute.

Not all of the subject provinces or districts were able to pay their tribute through agriculture and herding. In such cases other demands were made, such as those of the Chicha people mentioned above, in which the Incas tapped local rural resources for wild plants to be used as dyes, and medicines, as well as feathers, cactus spines, semi-precious stones and timber for building. For their own use the Andeans gathered locally eggs, and many wild plants for dyes, medicines, poisons, or charms.

Most Andeans kept swarms of guinea pigs in their houses, as a supply of meat to supplement their diet (69). Some people also kept dogs. Inca dogs were of medium size with a pointed face and a tightly curling tail, and were kept as pets (29) and scavengers, rather than for hunting, meat, or sacrifices.

69 Guinea pigs eating scraps (A reconstruction of coastal architecture by Dr Jiminez Borja)

8

Work and craftsmanship

In addition to rural work on the lands of the Religion and the Emperor, the commoners were expected to do manual work for the government in a number of different tasks. The main ways of paying the mit'a tax were, as already mentioned, to fight in the army, to serve in the public works force, working on building projects or in the mines. There were other tasks beside these, including repairing and servicing the bridges, tambos and Chasqui posts. (Since, however, the latter, according to Poma, were serviced by the sons of the curacas and officials this may not have been a 'mit'a' or work 'tax', but a more prestigious occupation.) Services to the Emperor and his officials, to the Religion and the priests, or to the curacas, which amounted to personal services of various kinds, were also included in this general category of work-tax.

SERVANTS

Servants and attendants worked in the houses of the Emperor, Religion, the nobility and all those whose positions merited such attentions, on a rota basis. The number of servants that any curaca or government official was served by depended on his status, on the number of householders in his responsibility. Ordinarily, one *mitayo* (servant) was appointed for 100 subjects governed; a Tocricoc Apu could expect to have about 400 servants.

Garcilaso tells us that there were attendants in the royal service such as sweepers, water-carriers, woodcutters, cooks for the courtiers' table, stewards, porters, keepers of the wardrobe and of the jewels, gardeners, overseers and other offices. Those who undertook many of these tasks did so not as individuals, but as respresentatives of certain villages, who were called upon to supply capable and faithful men in sufficient numbers to perform the duties. These servants then worked in spells of so many days, weeks, or months, which counted as tribute of their respective villages; any neglect was also the responsibility of the village and all the inhabitants were punished. The villages who supplied these servants were those nearest to Cuzco, within a radius of 15 to 20 kilometres (9 to 12 miles).

Other duties in serving the Emperor and the government were also assigned to particular villages all over the empire. The Emperor's dancers were men of Chumbavilcas; the Rucunas and the Soras were assigned to carry the Emperor's litter; those of Tambo were supposed to be a police force which enforced the law throughout the empire. Similarly, the Sapa Inca's imperial guard was drawn from men from the far-away province of Cañari, who were tied by bonds of loyalty to the Emperor and were not so easily swayed by the local political parties of Hanan and Hurin Cuzco, whose generals might be plotting a conspiracy.

Many of the personal servants to the Emperor came to be drawn from the *Yanacona*. These were often the survivors of provinces or villages who had fiercely resisted the Incas, or had behaved treacherously, rebelling against Inca rule. Pardoned from execution, they became full-time hereditary servants of the Inca. However, as time passed they became closely tied by loyalty to the Emperor, and were given positions of great prestige in his household—even in the government. An example of their loyalty in the reign of Huayna Capac was evidently recorded in Inca official historical narrative and comes to us through Murua: in the war with the Caranquis in Quito, Huayna Capac's guard of Inca nobles dropped his litter and fled when the Caranquis came out of their fortress to attack, but he was saved by the Yanacona who saw him lying on the ground. Back in Tomebamba Huayna Capac showed his displeasure to the nobles by withholding their rations while he heaped the Yanacona with gifts, preferring their company to that of all others. The expansion of the Yana class into a number of professions, such as herders looking after the Inca's animals, and as workers on the lands of the rulers, suggests that they were becoming an interesting new force in Inca society.

ARTISANS

Living in towns and capitals, there were those specially qualified artisans who produced luxury goods: gold- and silver-smiths, musicians, carpenters, lapidaries, also experts in weaving, embroidery and in building, who did special work for, and were employed by, the élite, mainly the Emperor and Religion, the curacas and governors. They were exempt from the usual tribute payments, and worked in a full-time professional craft for the members of the élite who supported them and their families in everything they needed, including tools and materials for their work. Admission to this class was usually hereditary, as with most other positions and classes in Inca society. References made in the records to fine craftsmanship do not, except in the case of architecture, name artists; rather, they emphasize the hereditary role of a tribal excellence in one or another craft such as the Chimu as goldsmiths or the Colla in stonework.

STONEWORKING AND QUARRYING

No references are made to artist sculptors, and what little sculpture the Incas produced was usually executed in wood. There are records of the Spanish priests destroying idols in the form of carved columns, but none of these now survive—unless the *Intihuatana* stones are included in this category (*71*). In the rare surviving examples of sculpture, we see that the style shrinks from representation, and as in architecture a feeling for mass, for planes, for functional form takes over. The most expressive form of stone-carving is found on the surfaces of caves and boulders, where terraced seats, steps, angular hollowing, channelling and other emphatic shapes were hewn out of solid rock (*70*), including—though only occasionally—a puma or a snake. In these carvings

70 Open air carvings in rock masses, Chinchero

71 Intihuatana stone, Machu Picchu

man appears to have been identifying himself with nature and creating his own shapes among those of the landscape. Aesthetically, the ingredients of sculpture were also included in the finest Inca masonry. The master stonemasons can be regarded as artists as well as craftsmen.

The stonemason's 'art' was an extremely important part of Inca architecture. These craftsmen were supported by the government and were sent to build the most important Inca buildings, the royal palaces and the Sun temples in the most favoured provincial capitals, and to instruct the natives in their craft. The stonemasons worked in close association with the mit'a force: 20,000 workers are reported to have worked annually on the great fortress of Sacsahuaman in the quarrying, transporting and building work; similar numbers of men were employed on other important building projects in the provinces.

Thousands of men worked in the quarries. Little is known about the methods or tools used in splitting off the granite and andesite blocks. It is thought that holes were bored, into which wooden wedges were inserted; water was then poured on, causing the expansion of the wedges and the splitting of the rock. The action of frost might have aided this method, but the area affected would have been more difficult to control. Possibly, great cross-bars were also employed. To bore the holes for the above method, by rapidly revolving a pestle-shaped stone or cane between the hands, using water and sand, would not have taken as long as might be imagined.

Stones were transported from the quarry to the site with the help of cables and wooden rollers. In the construction of Sac-sahuaman, and generally in the Cuzco region, three main types of stone, found in separate quarries, were used for their different characteristics. In the great fortress, giant blocks of Sacsahuaman diorite porphyry (some over 8 metres, or 26 ft, in height and width, and weighing over 200 tons) were used in the outer wall; these were found and hewn on the site.

The second type, a limestone from Yucay, some 15 kilometres (9 miles) away, was used for foundations. A third type of stone, a black andesite which weathers chocolate brown, used for the inside buildings, was brought from the relatively distant quarries of Huaccoto and Rumicolca, 15 and 35 kilometres (9 and 21 miles) respectively from Cuzco.

Great numbers of men were used in transporting the stones. Such feats were commemorated in legends recounting the dragging of 'weary stones'. These were particularly large blocks which would have caused the workers a great deal of weariness. One of the greatest of these, the Caicusa, was taken, according to Garcilaso, from a quarry '15 leagues away' on the other bank of the river Yucay. Of incredible size, it was hauled by 20,000 men, of whom it killed 3000, and finally, too 'tired' to mount the final slope, it was abandoned at the bottom of the Sacsahuaman hill.

Stoneworking tools were simple. Under the direction of the master-masons the stones were shaped with stone hammers, preferably of hematite. Sand and water were used for polishing when a smooth surface was desired. For measurement in fitting the blocks and spacing the architectural features, the Incas used body measurements. According to Rowe, they also knew of and used the sliding rule with arbitrary units of measurement and the plumb bob (76i). Bronze chisels may have helped in drilling holes in stone for some barholes and eye-bonders; but even the best bronze was too soft to last long in such work as finishing off their best stone work.

Two main types of masonry were perfected by the mason's

craft, and of these there were many variations for different purposes in building. The most monumental and sculptural style consisted of polygonal blocks, often huge (usually of limestone or diorite porphyry), used to construct great enclosure walls, the main retaining walls of terraces, and ramparts in fortresses as at Sacsahuaman (39). These large irregular blocks were shaped and fitted individually, each stone imperceptibly cupped by its support with extreme precision. They had great sculptural appeal in that their joints were recessed, so that a textural quality was achieved, at the same time the harshness of line was softened yet the massiveness accentuated by the play of light. Some blocks were cut with up to thirty-two angles, to which other blocks were fitted.

The second masonry style, the rectangular type (72), was quite different in character. Arranged in approximately regular courses, this type is found in its finest form in the temple of the Sun, Coricancha, cut almost without sunken joints, in black andesite blocks. Used in the finest palaces and temple buildings this style probably arose from the tradition of square-cut blocks of sod. Although the rectangular type was used in free-standing walls, in prominent locations it is found sometimes in retaining walls. Smaller cellular blocks, a variation of the polygonal type, were also used in temple and palace walls as well as in retaining walls (73), and sometimes both types of masonry appear in a single wall. Builders employed a combination of masonry styles, and types of stone, for articulation; a high correlation of the physical properties of the stones is found with the types of masonry styles, while the latter are also varied according to their functional strength.

Whereas the polygonal forms had to be carefully shaped and cut to match each other, the fitting of the rectangular types could be effected by the flat push-and-pull abrasion method, after the blocks had been approximately fitted. In each case the edges were then bevelled back to increase the 'dressed' effect of the smoothly finished, sunken joints. The weight of the stones in both polygonal and coursed masonry diminished with increasing height. In building the walls, levers and earth ramps were used: the heaviest stones were pulled up ramps built to the height of the wall on wooden rollers. The builders also used powerful little bronze crowbars, called *champis*, to get ashlars in place, which were too heavy to be lifted by hand. The bars were sufficiently strong to be

72 Stonemasonry: rectangular style in temple group Pisac
73 Polygonal or small cellular style used in the terrace and full-length niches of Colcampata, Cuzco

used in placing blocks of stone weighing 10–20 tons, and would have fitted into the small projections left on the stones, to lift them into place. These knobs were usually low on the block face and were sometimes left as decorative features instead of being chipped off.

Although the Inca builders knew of the technique which employed metal cramps, employed earlier in the Middle Horizon at Tiahuanaco, they rarely used it, except perhaps, in some blocks at Coricancha, and in a temple at Ollantaytambo—where the Spaniards destroyed the building searching for the 'gold which had been poured into the cracks' by the builders! On the contrary, the finest masonry was laid dry and not even a pin could be forced between the blocks. In the highlands these joints sometimes calcified in the damp weather—a feature which perhaps led to Spanish accounts of special 'glues', once used by the Incas. While blocks in some walls were carefully fitted in both inside and outside faces, the stones tapered slightly inside the wall and the cracks were filled with a little mud.

The engineering ingenuity of the master-masons is well illustrated by the use of keying, or locking, in a wall in the Torreon group, at Machu Picchu. Here a very experienced mason connected the Torreon, a semi-circular structure, with a two-and-a-half-storeyed house. The wall which united them is made of carefully selected and matched ashlars of white granite. Among the apparently rectangular blocks there are no mathematically correct right angles or straight lines. In time, the house at the southern end of the wall would have leant away from it, and the seams would have opened: to prevent this, the stonemasons ingeniously keyed the ashlars together at the point of greatest strain, by altering the pattern—from one which was virtually rectangular to one containing hook stones, thus making a series of braces which would prevent the ashlars from slipping and would prevent the house from leaning away.

Hammering with stone hammers and polishing with sand and water were also the techniques used to produce smaller stone objects such as axes, warclub heads, clod crushers, mortars, pestles, stone bowls, ceremonial dishes and figurines.

Plastically the best Inca sculpture consists of miniature figures of llamas and alpacas, pumas and human beings, carved of pre-grained stone, or even cast in bronze, silver or gold. These figures are very simple yet achieve formalized expression. The numerous small carvings of llamas and alpacas were executed in stones of different colours and textures, and had holes cut in their backs which would be filled with llama fat or coca as an offering (74). Rowe suggests that the finely carved stone dishes were similarly for ceremonial use—to catch the blood of sacrificed animals. Some of these bowls were very heavy, yet precisely

74 Alpacas and llama carved in stone

75 Ceremonial bowl carved in stone

balanced, of bold, unusual abstract shapes, finely grained and with a polished surface (*75*). Others were decorated with designs carved in relief, of pumas, snakes or in rare instances an incised scene.

METALLURGY AND MINING

In the Andean area, most of the metals available had been used for personal adornments or for religious offering and ceremonies since the Early Horizon, Chavin style. Copper weapons and tools also appeared soon after casting was introduced. Although bronze, an alloy made of copper and tin, had been discovered in Bolivia by *c.* AD 700 it was the Incas who were responsible for its wide and general use. Like all other Pre-Columbian Americans, the Andeans did not use iron. Iron does not occur pure in the ground and no evidence has shown, nor is likely to show, that the Incas knew how to smelt iron. Heavy metallic ores like hematite and meteoric iron could be utilized when these were found since they occur naturally.

Copper, tin, gold and silver were mined by the Incas and platinum was panned in Ecuador. All gold was confiscated by the government, a custom enforced by inspectors: 'As they esteemed silver and gold so highly, they ordered it mined in many parts of the provinces in great quantity.' Traders are even reported to have been sent out to look for possibilities for mining metals in newly conquered provinces.

Cieza tells us that when 'numbers of Indians were put to work in the mines, others were brought in to cultivate their fields', though we are told by another source that the mines were worked by labour from neighbouring provinces for a period of only four months a year, from noon to sunset, because of the inconvenience of the cold (in high altitudes).

> If one of the indians in the mines got sick, he was allowed to return home at once, and another came to take his place; but none was assigned to the mines unless he was married (a householder) so that his wives could look after his food and drink. . . . . Beside this they were permitted to stop several days in the month for their feasts and recreation. These indians were replaced by others after they had done their turn.

This quotation, taken from Cieza, shows a very different situation to descriptions of mine working under the Spanish, who drove the indians much harder, often until they dropped.

Due to the Spaniards' overpowering interest in precious metals, their observations are naturally centred on these. Three sorts of gold mines were mentioned by the chroniclers: The first type was the production of grains large enough to be collected without any further operation; secondly, dust or very small grains which had to be washed out and separated from the earth; and the third type, was of gold which was mixed with other metals or was embedded in rocks (other metals also being found in similar conditions). Pedro Sancho records the first eyewitness accounts of indians working in the mines near Chuquiabo:

> The mines are in the gorge of a river about half-way up the sides. They are made like caves, by whose mouths entry is made to scrape the earth, [which is done] with the horns of deer and was then carried outside in certain hides sewn into the form of sacks . . [of llama hide]. The manner in which they wash [the earth] is, they take a [jet] of water from the river, and on the bank they set up certain very smooth flag-stones on which they throw water . . . and the water [drawn off by a duct] carries off the earth little by little so that the gold is left upon the flag-stones themselves. . . . The mines go far into the earth . . . [between 20 and 40 metres] . . . a great mine which is called Huayna Capac goes into the earth some 80 metres. They have no light, nor are they broader than is necessary for one person to enter crouching down, and until the man who is in the mine

comes out, no other can go in. The people who get out the gold from here are as many as 50 . . . from one cacique come 20, from another 50, . . . according to the number they have. . . . guards [were placed] around the mines so that none of those who take out the gold can get away without being seen. At night when they return to their houses in the village, they enter by a gate where the overseers are who have the gold in their charge, and from each person they receive the gold he has got. There are other mines . . . scattered about through the land, which are like wells, a man's height in depth, so that the worker can just throw the earth from below on top of the ground.

This report was made by the first two Spaniards to investigate the Collao area, when they returned with a load of earth from which they obtained three pesos of gold. On this basis the Spaniards estimated that after instructing the indians in their more sophisticated mining techniques, they could obtain a million pesos of gold per annum!

The Andean indians' custom of revering all natural forces, landmarks, unusual objects or formations found in nature, is found also in their attitude to mining: ore deposits were considered to be shrines. Mountains which contained ore deposits, and the deposits themselves, were worshipped, and were presented with offerings. In addition, the Andeans prayed to them, and asked them to yield up their metal. In order to obtain more metal from these *huacas* (shrines or holy places), the miners drank and danced in religious ceremonies for their benefit. They not only worshipped the metals but praised the stones in which they were found.

The Incas smelted a variety of metals by the use of *huairas* (wind furnaces), cylindrical furnaces made of terracotta with a funnel of adobe bricks, about a metre high, with a series of openings along the sides. Crushed ore was placed with charcoal inside the huaira and ignited. The ores were smelted on hillsides where the huairas could capture air and the prevailing winds. The molten metal settled and was drained off at the base of the cylinder. Small crucibles were used in which to melt and refine metals. Bars of gold and silver were sent to Cuzco from Paria (Chile), Chuquiabo (La Paz), and Chuquisaca (La Plata), the provincial capitals in the centre of the most important mining districts. In many other provinces of the empire some metals were mined in smaller quantities. While tin sources were limited to southern areas, copper, silver and gold were much more widely distributed.

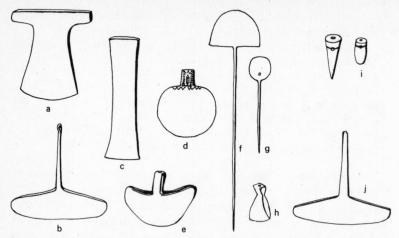

76 Cast metal objects: a *axe,* b & j *tumi knives,* c *chisel,* d *mirror,* e & h *tweezers,* f & g *tupu pins,* i *plumb bobs*

In working the metals the Incas demonstrated they appreciated their properties: Analyses of bronze tools have indicated that the metalworkers understood the effects of differing percentages of tin: hardness and mould-filling qualities. The high melting point of platinum they overcame by mixing grains of platinum with gold dust, repeatedly heating and hammering the mixture until it formed a mass (sintering).

The Chimu and Inca had a wider knowledge of different processes in metal technology than any other people in Pre-Columbian America. The techniques included many of those used today: hammering, annealing, casting in open and closed moulds, some primitive soldering, repoussé, gilding and even a type of plating. While many elaborate decorative pieces were made in a variety of techniques in the precious metals, it is in the use of copper and bronze, where the old forms of stone tools and weapons were copied in metals, that illustrate most clearly a continuity of the Andean culture with its native stone age.

Tools and weapon forms cast in copper and bronze particularly associated with the Incas are the flat, trapezoidal axe-blades with extensions for binding to a haft (*76*); and the *tumi* (knife) with a handle projecting at right angles to the blade. The decorated head was skilfully cast and an extension left for the knife. The cutting edges of the knives, axes and chisels were hammered and annealed for maximum hardness.

Cast Inca tools also included crowbars, bolas weights, warclub heads, mirrors, tweezers, needles and bells. The Incas knew the 'lost wax' method of casting which they probably learnt from the Chimu. Most Inca cast objects were of bronze and copper, but these included items which could also be made by different techniques and in other metals.

The lack of known Inca objects cast in gold and silver may be partly due to selection and their greater monetary value in post-Inca times. Gold and silver, used almost entirely for luxury goods and ceremonial objects, were usually worked by hammering the metal into thin sheets and repoussé ornamentation (77); stone hammers were used and when the metal became too brittle it was annealed by heating almost to the melting point so that its plasticity returned. The desired shape of an object could be achieved by cutting the sheet of metal or hammering it over a wooden form, to suggest volume. Decoration was also added by

77 *Silver alpaca found on the Island of Titicaca, 24 cms high*
78 *Standing female figure, cast silver, gold inlay, 25 cms high*
79 *Standing female figure of gold, 15 cms high*

hammering the back of a sheet to obtain a relief design on the face. Objects of sheet metal could be built up of several pieces by means of riveting. Small holes were usually drilled, but in a casting, larger holes were cast into the piece. Soldering was also used, the most common solder for small work being a finely pulverized copper oxide or copper carbonate mixed with some organic binder. The mixture was applied to the metal parts to be joined, and then reduced to metallic copper on the spot by means of flame and a blowpipe. The Incas may also have been familiar with the plating technique, the practise of which appears to have been restricted to the north coast region of Peru. However, incrustation and inlay, both of different materials and of one metal in another, were practised by the Incas. Some known pieces include shell in silver, silver in bronze, lead in wood, lacquer separated by gold wires (cloisonné) in silver. A rare example of solid casting in a silver and gold admixture occurs in a male figurine, inlaid with Venus shell, spondulux and gold. In fig. 78 a silver casting of a figurine is inlaid with gold.

Objects in gold and silver were made for and used by the Sapa Inca, the nobility and the Religion. Gold was the symbolic colour of the Sun and the Sapa Inca, and silver that of the Moon and the Coya. Some descriptions of gold work on temple and palace walls and in gardens have already been quoted (pp.131, 133); the following one is taken from Cieza:

Treasure in [a Sapa Inca's house] piled up over many years so that all the service of the ruler's house, even water jars and kitchen utensils, was of gold and silver: and not only in a single place, but in many, especially the capitals of the provinces, where there were many gold and silversmiths engaged in the manufacture of these objects. In their palaces and lodgings there were bars of these metals, and their garments covered with ornaments of silver, emeralds and turquoise, and other precious stones of great value. And for their wives there was even greater luxury in their adornment and for their personal service, and their litters were all encrusted with silver and gold and jewels . . . and as they observed and held to that custom of burying treasure with the dead, it is easy to believe . . . incredible quantities of it were placed in their graves.

. . . Even their drums and [stools] and musical instruments and arms were of this metal and to glorify their state . . . it was a law that none of the gold and silver brought into Cuzco could be removed, under penalty of death.

For personal decoration bangles and sequins were sewn on clothing, *tupu* pins were made for fastening women's garments, there were pendants to be hung around the neck, bracelets for awards, and earrings. Gold and silver objects were distributed by the Emperor as gifts. In addition, small but formally dynamic figurines representing women, men, llamas, alpacas and other animals have been found, which had been used as offerings at shrines. A small standing figurine, with arms tightly folded across the chest, has recently been found in its original state in a burial, wrapped in mantles and its face showing below a headdress of red feathers. This context suggests these figures (79) were 'dolls' to be dressed and not intended as figurines of particular artistic merit.

BONE, SHELL, WOOD AND GOURDS

Llama bone was the most accessible material for the making of bone tools and implements, which included spoons, needles, weaving picks, spindle whorls, flutes and beads. There were other more ornamental purposes in the use of bone, and several pieces of bone might be carved to make up figurines. Shell was used mainly for inlay work, for beads and for small human and animal figurines, whether as jewellery or offerings.

Wood, although a limited resource in some parts of the Andean area, was used by the Incas for a number of essential purposes. Large timbers were imported, as tribute from forested regions, and stored in Cuzco to be used as roof frames, parts of looms for weaving cloth, litters, axe handles, warclubs, knuckle-dusters, syringe tubes, digging sticks and hoes, also spoons, cups and ear-spools decorated with feathers. Wood was also carved especially for sacrificial purposes, in the form of human figures. Tomb posts, in the form of agricultural implements and wooden staffs of office, ornately carved and decorated with paint and metal sheathing, have also been found preserved on the coast. Since they were found only in Inca-period burials and are referred to in the records, these may be added to the list of Inca wood carving.

Artistically the most important woodwork was in the form of cups, and the professional woodworkers were called *Kero-Camayoc*, (Cup Specialists). In Quechua, these cups are called *kero*. Simple solid forms, shaped like tumblers but wider at the mouth than at the base, the kero held from 0.14 (1 quart) to 1.9 litres (2 quarts) of chicha maize beer. Decoration consisted of geometric patterns of incised lines, or a pattern of small holes, which could be inlaid with lead. Cut designs, of simple floral motifs, were filled with coloured lacquer, fastened in by a vegetable gum. These cups, usually used in pairs, played an important role in community life since they were used for ceremonious toasting, and when entertaining guests or acquaintances.

Later, in the colonial period, the designs became much more figurative, lively lacquer painted scenes showing a mixture of Spanish and Inca customs and ideas. The drawings of the figures are animated and the painting executed in a range of bright colours. The development of this interesting art form in the post-Inca period may well have been due to the fact that the Spaniards monopolized the supply of gold, so that the Inca élite were deprived of their golden tumblers.

Gourds were not produced in the highlands and were not generally used by the Incas. Some, however, obtained from the warmer lands where they were grown, were used to a limited extent for measures of volume; but pottery served for all pots and most containers.

POTTERY

Standard Inca pottery forms and designs are considered to be those from the homeland area around Cuzco, and are recognized by archaeologists as 'Cuzco Inca'. Good clays for pottery and temper are abundant near Cuzco, and are also locally available in most parts of the Andean area, although they vary in quality. The best-known ancient pottery works near Cuzco was at San Sebastian, at a distance of about 5 kilometres (3 miles).

The Cuzco Inca pottery was well made by hand, without any mechanical aids. The potter's wheel was unknown in Ancient America, and mass-produced mould-made pottery was a regional speciality of the Chimu in the Andean area. Inca pottery is fine-grained, very hard, and finished with a highly polished surface. The surfaces of the paste were usually oxidized (fired in an open pit or furnace where the air circulated) to a pinky-red or orange colour, the centre usually remaining slightly grey. The surfaces of most vessels, except for cooking pots, were decorated with slip paint (liquid clay solution) to which mineral pigments were added for some of the colours obtained—white, cream, purple, red and black. These vessels, called 'Cuzco Polychrome', were painted with repetitive geometric designs:

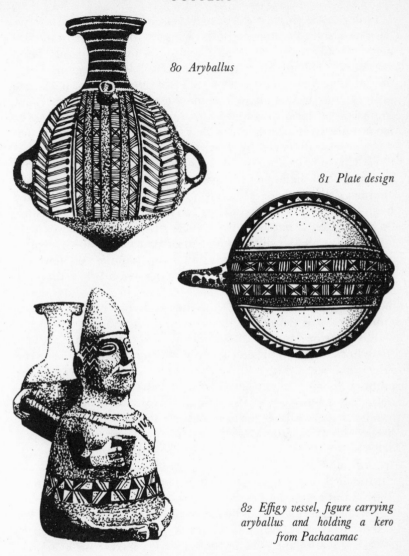

80 Aryballus

81 Plate design

82 Effigy vessel, figure carrying aryballus and holding a kero from Pachacamac

diamonds, chequers, and cross-hatching. Triangles, and parallel stripes of varied thickness, are also common motifs, used in bands on the body of a vessel or as articulation following the rim. A highly stylized motif representing plant life was organized on a vertical stem-line, from which project diagonal rows of two or three parallel lines, each ending in a knob (*80*).

Other more highly decorated vessels, on which attractive designs of stylized animals, birds or insects are painted in rows or geometrically arranged in patterns, often include the use of an orange slip colour, introduced from the Titicaca region. There are other regional influences which occasionally appear in Inca pottery, but it was more common for Inca prototypes to be imitated for local use and distribution in the provinces (by local potters), resulting in a wide variety of Late Horizon styles, more or less influenced by the prestigious Inca ware.

In Cuzco, a wide variety of elegant standard shapes were designed for functional effectiveness. The best known and most characteristic of these is the aryballus jar, which has a pointed base, a long neck with flaring lips and small lugs (*80*), which could be topped by a flat lid with a high strap handle; it was used for carrying and storing liquids. In order to carry the aryballus on the back there were two small strap handles, set low and vertically on the vessel's body, and also a knob below the neck around which a rope could be passed (*82*). The aryballus jar was made in many sizes, ranging from the height of a human figure to miniatures used for offerings.

The plate or flat dish was another typical shape. It had either a small horizontal handle on each side, or a modelled handle on one side and a pair of lugs on the other. The dish was decorated with painted design elements adapted to the circular form (*81*). Jugs, bottles and bowls were also common (*16*). Covers with looped handles were available for most of these shapes. Another ceramic shape, the drinking cup, is similar to that of the wooden kero, decorated with geometric designs and painted most prominently around the rim.

Modelled ornament was another facet of pottery decoration. Plate handles might be modelled in the shape of bird heads (especially ducks), human heads, or just knobs; puma heads were also used as motifs for handle knobs or, in a more stylized form, as aryballus knobs, and eyes and noses were added to neck jars.

Cooking pots, which were made of hard, plain brown ware, were not painted and were decorated only with simple modelled snakes applied on the body, or with buttons. Cooking-pot shapes consisted mainly of a pedestalled bowl with a broad horizontal loop handle and a flat lid and handle. The pedestal bowls show a great variation of outline, some more rounded, some squatter or more angular. Also common were cooking braziers with a wide opening at the side and three solid cylindrical feet (*16*).

The standard Inca wares have been found widely distributed throughout the empire, and were used in all the larger towns and tambos; but fewer have been found in small settlements, where only a government official or curaca was usually able to acquire them. More crudely made local wares were in use, side by side with the prestigious Inca ware, some of whose characteristics were copied. Particularly on the coast the aryballus occurs in interesting variations, and realistic modelling is added to Inca forms as in fig. 82 where a figure holds a kero and carries the aryballus on his back.

Other ceramic artefacts were few, consisting of dice, spindle whorls and spoon ladles.

WEAVING AND TEXTILES

Although few Inca textiles have survived the damp highland climate, some fragments of cloth have been preserved in burials and many more are available from the coastal regions of the empire. Due to the dry climate of the coast, some examples of Inca weaving have also been preserved intact.

Wool, the main source for highland cloth, was available in several shades of brown, black and white, from the cameloids, and in small quantities from the coats of the viscacha and bats. Also, in the hot lands cotton was grown in six natural colours and was available to the Incas. The quality of the wool was graded: the vicuñas' fleece was used to weave the finest clothing, the alpaca rated second and provided the bulk of the standard wool, while the llamas' coarse fleece was used mainly for cords and woven bags for transporting supplies. Vegetable and possibly mineral dyes were used extensively, the brightest colours appearing in wool, which, due to its structure, takes strong dyes better than cotton. Young girls gathered plants for dyes[1] and the raw material was dyed before the fibres were spun. Women spun wool at all times of the day, between their other tasks and even as they walked or relaxed. Fibres were spun clockwise on slender spindle shafts by hand. A distaff, a stick with a fork at the top, held the wool, or the latter could be wound around the wrist. The thread was pulled out by the right hand while the spindle hung free, or was played like a yoyo as the thread was twisted and tied onto it (*31*). Some threads measured two or three times the fineness of modern machine threads. Single threads were used, but more often two or more were twisted together anticlockwise before weaving.

The thickness of threads varied according to the item to be woven. For blankets very thick threads were used: the coarsest thread, called *cosi*, was sometimes 1 cm. thick in the weft. The *awasqua* was cloth used for normal clothing, woven by a householder's wife for everday wear. Examples found of this cloth show it was often woven plain or might have simple weft-and-warp stripes and geometric patterns inserted by additional warp colour-threads. Fine Inca tapestry cloth, called *cumbi*, was woven in many colourful and ornate patterns, usually in the tapestry technique. Such textiles could be elaborated by the use of floats, skipping threads in pattern form, leaving a floating pattern into which additional coloured threads could be embroidered or woven. Inca textiles were not usually embroidered, but feathers were frequently tied in with the weft elements, or sewn in, and were particularly favoured by the Incas, who imported colourful feathers from the jungle to sew into large feathered shirts and capes.

It can be assumed that the Incas had some knowledge of the pre-*Inca* weaving and textile techniques. The ancient Peruvians practised every technique known to handloom weavers anywhere in the world. The most elaborate woven and embroidered textiles found, in the Paracas peninsula on the Peruvian coast, date back to 100 BC and surpass any others known. In the Inca period the finest cloth, called *cumbi*, was woven by professional weavers and women in the Acllahuasi, for the Emperor, Religion and the élite. In a society where textiles were continually being woven for garments to be worn at important occasions, and where dress denoted social and official rank, the designs and techniques had become somewhat standardized. Only the élite wore or used the elaborately woven and embroidered mantles, like those used as grave goods made more than 1,000 years earlier. Men were probably responsible for making the heavier cloths, such as quilted or padded army wear.

The elaborate techniques known by the ancient Peruvians included tapestry (slit and interlocking techniques) and kelim tapestry. Embroidery was executed with flat, chain, loop or stem stitches, constructed like network, but on a fabric foundation. Floats were used in tapestry and in gauze weave. The latter was a speciality of the Chancay region on the coast, c. AD 1000–1532. Here the warps were crossed and wrapped round each other in attractive lacy patterns and included both abstract and figurative designs. The brocade technique, in which coloured designs are added by welt threads, and double cloth were also woven by the ancient Peruvians. In the double-cloth technique, two textiles are woven at the same time on a single loom with warps interwoven at certain points, so that the pattern reverses; there are also examples of triple and even quadruple cloths. Patchwork, or scaffolding (not done on a proper loom) and tie-dyeing were known since early times. The batik technique, in which areas of resist wax reject the dye, was used mainly on the coast. A form of simple crochet and an elementary knitting stitch were also used. The non-weaving techniques of netting, braiding, crocheting and knitting are also found, used singly or in combination, with weaving for finishing borders.

Ancient fabrics show that the patterns of dress had already been developed by Paracas Cavernas times. Cloth was woven in already usable shapes, rectangular or slightly flared with additional warps (or wefts) (*83*).

The back-strap loom was also in use over 2,000 years before the Inca period and was generally used throughout the Andean area. It consisted of two parallel rods which supported the warp threads: at one end, it fastened onto a post, or projecting peg or branch, and at the other end a belt attached to the second rod passed around the waist of the weaver. The weaver, who usually sat, could vary the tension by moving his or her body (*31*). Another type of loom which stood upright was also used by the Incas.

83 Woven shapes were usually rectangular but some variation could be obtained by tightening the weave (wefts) or by adding warp threads for widening the cloth

84 Inca shirt, wool, 95 cms by 80 cms

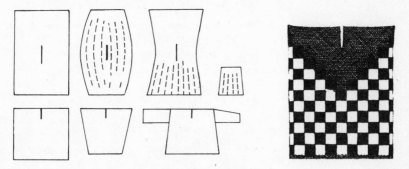

Consisting of a vertical frame of four poles, built against a wall, this type of vertical loom was used for the production of wide cumbi cloth.

Mention has already been made of Inca dress and design motifs in cloth (p. 34). While some Inca shirts had small repetitive geometric designs, in others, colour areas were large, broad and intense (*84*). In their choice of colours it is evident that the Incas preferred more artificial and sophisticated colours than the warm natural colours favoured by the earlier cultures. While many fine pieces are masterpieces of precisely planned design, calculated to fit the shape of the shirt, others are less successful. In featherwork, bright colours and the texture and lustre of the feathers, may give a unified appearance to some designs which are poorly integrated, showing a certain lack of flexibility in the medium.

Some textiles were also ornamented with metalwork. Figures cut out of thin sheets of hammered gold and silver were sewn on cloth in patterns. Round gold bangles, which may have been sewn on cloth, have also been found.

In basketing and matting the *Inca* were technically expert but treated these entirely as utility objects and seem to have had little interest in decorating them.

1. Dyes were obtained in three main primary colours and the wool was then given successive dyeings to mix these: blue and yellow, red and blue, yellow and red, produced greens, violets and oranges; also the variation of the natural wool and cotton colours could be employed to vary the tone or shade of the dye results.

    A variety of celestial to deep *blues* were probably obtained by immersion in light or deep indigo baths. A fabric, yellow when removed from an indigo bath becomes blue with the oxidizing action of the air.

    Red came from vegetable and animal sources. The best known source is *cochineal*, produced by a beetle and gathered from the leaves of the *Opuntia* cactus. Cochineal produces a slightly carmine red, or black—according to the mordant used.

    Yellow may have come from the bark of the *Chinus mollis* (false pepper tree) but other substances were probably also known.

    (Based on D'Harcourt)

9

Religious life

In pre-*Inca* times a few important deities, numerous idols and sacred places were worshipped by the Andean peoples and many of these survived Inca domination. It was Inca policy to permit subject provinces considerable religious freedom, so long as the people complied with the demands made on them by Inca religious authority. In fact, the deities worshipped by the Incas were superimposed on the local pantheon of gods, which had to cede first place to them. But where the Incas encountered ancient and widely known oracles or shrines, they showed them respect, even worshipping and consulting such oracles themselves.

According to Cieza, 'Incas believed there was a Creator of all things and the Sun was their sovereign god, to whom they erected great temples . . . they gave importance to the immortality of the soul and other secrets of nature.' Inca religion, however, in its general application to everyday life in the empire, was not primarily concerned with the spiritual life of individuals, or with mysticism. Rather, it was organized to serve more practical ends which were complementary to economic and social policies reflecting the reality of Inca power.

It should not be assumed, however, that the practical orientation of Inca Religion meant a lack of religious involvement on the part of the people. On the contrary, underlying the carefully structured religious theory, was a recognition of the highly superstitious nature of the Andean people. The individual had to ensure his, or her, well-being by carefully carrying out all the prescribed ritual requirements and by observing every detail of respectful worship. This was to ensure the benevolence of all the forces whose power was believed to be expressed in the many aspects of the environment. Any misfortune or adversity experienced by an individual, whether physical or economic, was seen as punishment by the supernatural forces for some lapse in attention, as well as for a wrong committed.

The relationship of the Incas to their deities, and the relative importance of these deities in the Inca period, is expressed by Pachacuti Yamqui's cosmological diagram (*85*) simplified in the model (*86*). In this model Viracocha, the Creator, was both father and mother of the Sun and Moon, while Viracocha was also referred to by Pachacuti Yamqui as the 'Real Sun'. In the model the Sun and Moon produced Venus, as the 'Morning Star', and to Venus, the 'Evening Star'; the Morning Star was then father to Cama Pacha (Lord Earth) from whom man descended, and the Evening Star was mother to Mama Cocha (Lady Ocean) from whom woman descended.

VIRACOCHA

The nature of this deity is hard to assess: in fact, the term was commonly used in such varied contexts that it should perhaps be regarded more in the nature of a phenomenon, than a clearly defined single godhead.

Sarmiento tells us that the natives affirmed that in the beginning, Viracocha created a dark world without Sun or Moon; these were created later, along with the Thunderbolt, the Stars, the Earth and the Sea, and finally men, who were created in his own likeness. Viracocha, who was 'bearded', was then believed to have walked through the land as a bearer of culture, until he came to Manta, where he disappeared over the sea. This journey ranges just beyond the limits of the earlier Tiahuanaco-Huari empire and Cieza identifies Ticci Viracocha as the great pre-*Inca* god connected with Tiahuanaco. Cieza (as well as other sources) also confirms the existence of an important temple and idol to Viracocha in the village of Cacha, remains of which can be seen today. Here, Viracocha was said to have caused a volcano to erupt as a sign of his 'displeasure' with the ways of men. However, Inca accounts also emphasize the point the Viracocha was an unknown quantity — 'invisible' — of which the Sun was the chief visible representation. The Incas, in this view, did not build temples to house his image since he was too elusive. But we find that the Incas worshipped at some pre-*Inca* temples associated with his cult, for instance at Pachacamac; they also communicated with Viracocha from Huanacauri, and built the temple at Cacha to house an image of him, carved in stone; another image

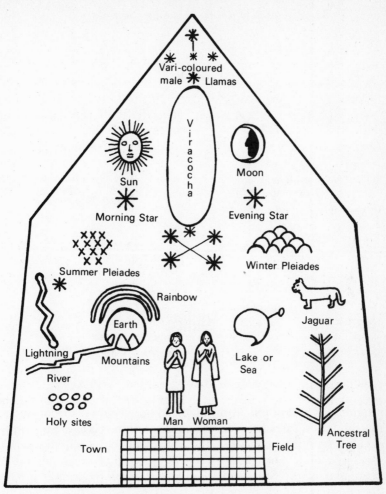

Vari-coloured male Llamas

Viracocha

Sun

Moon

Morning Star

Evening Star

Summer Pleiades

Winter Pleiades

Rainbow

Jaguar

Earth

Lightning

Mountains

Lake or Sea

River

Holy sites

Man   Woman

Town

Field

Ancestral Tree

85 The position of the Inca deities on the wall of the Temple of the Sun, Coricancha, Cuzco. (Based on the diagram by Pachacuti Yamqui)

of Viracocha was in the shape of a man and was placed in the Coricancha, Cuzco. Finally, Poma records that Inca Pachacuti tried to make the Creator supersede the earlier Sun worship of the *Inca*.

As Zuidema suggests, the concept of Viracocha, the Creator, could possibly be explained as being, to the Incas at least, a relatively theoretical construct. For instance, Murúa records that Capac Yupanqui, the fifth Inca, asked his councillors to solve a

86 A model of the diagram (After Zuidema)

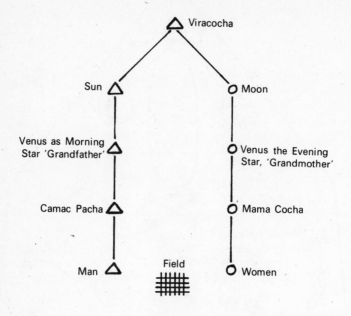

religious or philosophical problem: Who was most important—the Sun or Viracocha? After long discussion, Capac Yupanqui decided on Viracocha since the Sun could be obscured by the smallest cloud. The Incas were quite aware of the predictable behaviour of the Sun, and, therefore, the inference that it was under orders. Murúa records that it was the Inca Capac Yupanqui who made an elegant hymn to the Creator, saying how he formed and painted men and women and that it was during his reign that the miracle of the volcanic eruption took place at Cacha! Zuidema, however, sees the placing of Viracocha above the Sun as an expression of a moiety contrast and not a generally applicable view. The Sun temple of the Hanan rulers was located in Hurin Cuzco, and the temple of Quishuarcancha, the centre for the priests who were traditionally from Hurin Cuzco, was in Hanan Cuzco (p.115).

The elements of contrast between Viracocha and the Sun are

as follows: the Sun is connected with the sky, fire, and mountain country. Viracocha is connected with the earth, water, and the coast. In this view Zuidema sees the contrast between the Sun and Viracocha, and between Hanan and Hurin, as connected by the *Inca* with the contrast of heaven and earth, and of mountain to coastal regions, although there is no evidence that the coastal people felt themselves to be the inferiors of the mountain people, as a logical consequence of this.

THE SUN

Within the official Inca state religious organization the Sun traditionally headed the active deities. As the divine ancestor of the Inca dynasty the Sun's role within this organization was dominant, and associated with Inca prestige and power.

The study of the Sun's movements by the Inca astronomers, and the twelve-month calendar are traditionally closely linked with agricultural practice. The worship and cult of the Sun and observation of 'his' movements were of utmost importance to a people whose organization was founded on an agricultural economy (p. 197). The Sun in the cold highlands was the 'Giver of Life', whose presence transformed the environment, bringing about the maturing of the vital crops, not least that of the maize cobs.

The principal Inca temples for the cult of the Sun were built by the government throughout the empire. In each area, some land was given over to support of religious officials and attendants, as grazing for llamas and for growing maize to be used in rituals and as offerings. These lands were called 'lands of the Sun' and while the Sun cult absorbed most of the produce, other cults, including local cults, varying in proportion to their importance, were also supported from these lands. In reality, as suggested by Cobo, they should be thought of as the lands of 'Religion', which were divided between the various cults. The convents of the Sun Virgins and Chosen Women, called Acllahuasi, were also supported out of the proceeds of the lands for Religion.

The main temple of the Inca religion was the Coricancha, in Cuzco, and within its largest and richest shrine was kept the image of the Sun 'of great size and made of gold'. Several images of the Sun were known (at least two fell into Spanish hands) and these are described as representing the Sun by a huge golden disc—the size of a man, with rays radiating from a human face. Sarmiento

87 Temple of the Three Windows in the Sacred Plaza, Machu Picchu
88 Detail of two of the windows

tells us that Pachacuti Inca had two other images of gold made for the Coricancha: One, called *Viracocha Pachayachachi*, represented the Creator and was placed on the right of the image of the Sun; the other, *Chuqui ylla*, which represented the image of the God of Thunder, and was placed on the left of the Sun.

In most provincial capitals Sun temples were built with no mention of the Creator, and in these the Sun was served by the other sky gods. However, Murúa records that when Huayna Capac went to live in Tomebamba with his court, he built shrines as follows:

. . . and [Huayna Capac] built there the houses of the Creator, the Sun and the Thunder, as in Cuzco, and he gave them lands, servants, and herds in the same order and manner kept in Cuzco, and further-more he put the principal 'huaca' which was most venerated and respected in Cuzco, called Huanacaure, and also all the other huacas in the areas of Cuzco, all in the same order and design as they kept them in Cuzco, and in the plaza he built the edifice for the usnu, which the indians called Chuquipillaca [earthquake], to sacrifice the chicha to the Sun when he drank with him.

Important rituals associated with Inca ancestor-worship and other important ceremonies took place in the Huacapata, the Holy Plaza of Cuzco. The fortress of Sacsahuaman is also fre-quently referred to as a 'House of the Sun'. This religious aspect is perhaps symbolic, representing Inca power, especially since the fortress was also described as the 'House of the Inca', and one of its towers as Sunturhuasi.

THE THUNDER GOD

Thunder was regarded as the servant and messenger of the Sun. In the highlands his worship was associated with the represen-tation of Venus as the Morning Star. The Thunder, or God of Weather, was called *Ilyap'a* or *Illapa* (a word which incorporates the ideas of thunder, lightning and thunderbolt). Prayers for rain were addressed to him. It rained, as the poem on p. 49 suggests, when he broke the rain jug held by his sister. Cobo describes him as a man made up of the stars in the sky, holding a warclub in one hand and a sling in the other. His garments shone, resplendent with lightning as he turned to take a shot with his slingstone—and it was with the thunder of the shot that he shattered the water jar, causing rain. Since the presence of this deity was felt everywhere, shrines for his worship were widely distributed. Special sacrifices were made to this god and communi-cation was made with him from the highest places.

Pachacuti Inca adopted *Inti Illapa* (Thunderbolt) for his own personal *guanqui* (guardian or 'brother'), because it had appeared,

89 Masonry shrine inside the Temple of the Moon, near Machu Picchu

spoken to him and had given him a serpent with two heads as his insignia and to preserve him against misfortune. He carried this insignia with him to war.

THE MOON AND THE STARS

Complementary to the male Sun was *Mama-Quilla* (Mother Moon). While the Inca Emperor was the representative of the Sun on earth, his sister-wife, the Coya, was associated with the Moon. The Moon was represented as female and was important in calculating the months and in regulating the festival calendar. She was worshipped in a separate shrine to that of her husband the

90 Acllahuasi at Pachacamac

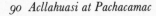

Sun, whom she served. Her shrine, ornamented with silver, was served by priestesses.

The Stars, of which Venus was the chief representative, were viewed as the children of the Sun and the Moon. They and the constellations were worshipped in the belief that they tended everything that had been created. For instance, each species of bird and animal was thought to be protected by a patron; groups of stars were also regarded as the patrons of certain activities. The Pleiades (*Collca*, meaning granary) were recognized by communities and families everywhere, since they were believed to watch over the preservation of seed. Another group of stars, the Lira or Cross (*Urcuchillay*—a vari-coloured llama), was respected by the herders who believed it was responsible for the conservation of the herds. *Catachillay*, another llama, slightly smaller, accompanied Urcuchillay.

THE EARTH AND THE SEA

Pacha-mama (Mother Earth), a female deity, was associated with agriculture. She was represented by a long-shaped stone which was placed in the fields, was worshipped, and asked to protect and fertilize the fields. The larger the fields or property she occupied, the more importance and respect she was accorded. The Coya, in her role of Mama Huaco (Manco Capac's mother) was the patroness of agriculture, and it was traditionally Mama Huaco's field that was cultivated first each August, at the beginning of the agricultural year.

The closeness of the relationship between the Coya and Mother Earth is illustrated by Murúa's account, in which he describes how Huayna Capac set up his mother's mummy as an oracle for Pacha-mama in Tomebamba.

Mama-cocha, Mother of the lakes and of water in the highlands, and of the sea on the coast, was worshipped mainly by the fishermen of the coast.

LOCAL BELIEFS AND HUACAS

Supernatural forces associated with places and objects were referred to as *huacas* (holy sites). The 'Relacion de los Ceques', in Cobo's chronicle, lists and describes the huacas in their distribution around Cuzco. The Relacion describes over 350 holy sites, conceived in groups on lines each of which radiated from the centre of Cuzco. Each imaginary line was called a *ceque*. Huacas were also set up by Huayna Capac at Tomebamba, which followed those in the Cuzco plan, and similar ceque systems may have radiated from other highland towns. In Cuzco, the maintenance of the huacas lying on these ceque lines, was assigned to respective social groups into which the population of the town was divided, and which in some cases can be identified.

The huacas listed for Cuzco can be summarized as follows: temples, cult objects, tombs of ancestors, stones, fountains, springs, calendar markers, hills, bridges, houses and quarries; also listed are places referred to in Inca mythology, or associated with past Inca Emperors, such as Huancauri, caves, hills, stones, meeting places and battlefields. The diagram of the ceque system (*91*) shows the division of Cuzco's ceques into geographical regions representing the four great quarters of the empire. There were nine ceque respectively in the three quarters of Chinchaysuyu, Antisuyu and Collasuyu. These nine ceque lines were subdivided into three groups of three, called *Collana* (a), *Payan* (b), and *Cayao*

91 Diagram of the Ceque system and solar towers (After Zuidema)

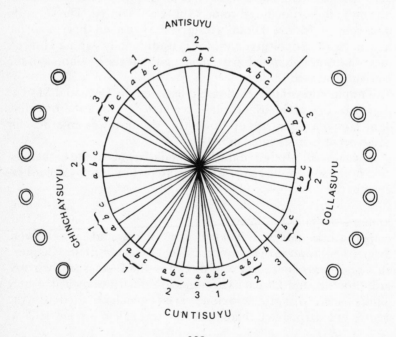

(c). In Cuntisuyu the number of ceque lines was increased to 14. In the territory bounded by each group of three ceques, the chroniclers mention one panaca and one ayllu in connection with Payan and Cayao. It may therefore be that the ruler-founders of the panaca were linked to the Collana ceque of the same group to which their panaca were linked. It has been proposed by Zuidema that the principles of organization found in the religious ceque system may also be fundamental to the social and political organization in Cuzco and so of the empire.

Huanacauri, the most important huaca, was distinguished from the sky gods by most chroniclers, and was described as 'a spindle--shaped unwrought stone' situated on Huanacauri hill, near Cuzco. The hill was also associated, by Sarmiento, with the rainbow and can be seen as an example of the mountain representing a celestial deity. According to an origin myth, the stone represented Ayar Uchu, one of Manco Capac's brothers, who was a special patron of religion for the Inca family and youths. For this reason, it played a prominent part in Inca rituals and the maturity rites, at which times the royal family visited the shrine for special ceremonies; some sources confirm that the Incas also came here to worship the Creator. Other mountains near Cuzco were also believed to be important deities, whose supernatural powers were usually estimated in proportion to their height.

Ayar Cachi, 'Lord of the Land', another of Manco Capac's brothers, was believed to have been turned into stone on the location of the future Sun temple when he symbolically took possession of Cuzco. Similar stone pillars were generally regarded as huacas and as guardians of the fields. Boundary-markers called *Saywa* were also regarded as huacas, as were piles of stones, called *apacita*, which marked dangerous or important places in the roads. In fact, anything or anybody that was dead, unusual or in some way awe-inspiring, could be called huaca, and be worshipped. Small portable images and amulets, representing humans, animals, plants, etc., which were of unusual shape or coloured stone and crystal, were also called huaca and were used for personal protection. The Inca Emperor had such a guardian, called his *guanqui* or 'brother', which he said protected and advised him. In the case of Pachacuti Inca this took the form of the Thunderbolt who appeared to him in a dream, but Manco Capac and Mayta Capac both chose the Inti bird.

PRIESTS AND PRIESTESSES

The high priest in Cuzco was the head of the hierarchy of priests in the empire. He was called *Uillac Uma* (the Highest Priest). However, the Emperor himself was the chief custodian of the Sun, and visited the temples, oracles and their estates. The high priests of the temple in Cuzco probably all belonged to the panaca of the Inca Viracocha's descendants (or Lloque Yupanqui's lineage), or they were closely related to the Inca. Under the high priest, Blas Valera recorded, there were *Hatun Uillca*, each of whom was head of one of the ten dioceses into which the country was divided, and who were rather like bishops. Under the Hatun Uillca there were *Yana Uillca*, the ordinary priests.

Cobo says that the high priest held that post for life, that he was married, and that he was so revered that he competed in authority with the Sapa Inca. He had power over all shrines and temples, to which he appointed priests. The hierarchical order of the priests probably varied, as in the case of the curacas, corresponding to the importance of the shrine. Large shrines may have been attended by priests of various ranks with duties covering a wide spectrum of activities: divining, interpreting oracles, hearing confessions and prescribing penances, praying, interceding for the dead, performing sacrifices, presiding over a variety of rituals; also diagnosing and treating diseases. There were titles for most of these duties, but it is not known how specialized the priests were. At least, at small shrines a single priest or caretaker must have had a wide range of duties, and at shrines of limited local importance, the family or ayllu concerned supplied and supported an attendant, usually an old man, to look after the huaca.

While male priests officiated at most shrines, priestesses were sometimes given positions of high authority. In the pre-*Inca* temple of Wari-wilka, in the province of Jauja, an important idol, consisting of a tree adorned with golden breasts and in female attire, was attended by a priestess called *Sarpay*. Priestesses in Cuzco, and in other Inca temples, were responsible for serving the shrine of the Moon and carrying her silver image. But a group of Chosen Women were also consecrated to generally serving in the Sun temples and formed an order under a high priestess. This high priestess was chosen for her high birth from among the Sun Virgins of royal blood, in the Acllahuasi. The priestesses were sworn to a life of chastity, but the priests may have been allowed to marry, as in the case of the high priest.

THE ACLLAS AND THE MAMACUNAS

In Cuzco many of the Acllas were the daughters of the leading nobles, while elsewhere they were chosen from the surrounding province by the Apupanaca. On arrival in the Acllahuasi the young girls were looked after and educated by the Mamacunas (p. 77). After their presentation at Cuzco to the Emperor, they were divided into three main categories: those to be given to men, those to serve Religion (particularly the cult of the Sun), and those to educate the next generations of Acllas in the convents. Poma describes six categories of ordinary virgins and six categories of virgins of the idols. These categories may represent age groups, but probably existed side-by-side with an hierarchical order expressed in different types of duties. Such duties included serving various idols or shrines, dyeing, spinning and weaving cumbi cloth for the Inca and the Sun (the Emperor, and for Religious sacrifices), the making of chicha and preparation of food for sacrifices, and the education of the Acllas.

Sarmiento wrote a description of one of Pachacuti's visits to the temple of the Sun when he watched the Mamacunas serve the Sun's dinner:

> This was to offer much richly cooked food to the image or idol of the Sun, and then to put it into a great fire on an altar. The same order was taken with the liquor. The chief of the Mama-cunas saluted the Sun with a small vase, and the rest was thrown on the fire. Besides this many jars full of that liquor were poured into a trough which had a drain, all being offerings to the Sun.

The chastity of the Acllas and Mamacunas was of utmost importance and fiercely guarded. Poma describes the punishments meted out for any lapses: both parties were hung by the hair from a cliff or tree until they died, but even when an Aclla was forced she received 50 lashes with a rope with a stone at its end, and ended up half-dead.

WORSHIP

Mocha, the gesture of reverence before a deity or before the Emperor, consisted of a low bow from the waist with arms outstretched above the level of the head. With a labial click, the worshipper brought his open hands to his lips and kissed his fingertips. Sometimes, for a show of additional reverence, a switch was also held.

Prayers and communication with the gods could be made silently, aloud or with gestures. Reverence was paid to water sources, fields of the Sun, mountains and other important landmarks in many simple ways, such as by the addition of a stone to the *apacita* (pile of stones). Standard phrases could be uttered as prayers or could be made up, or priests and friends could be asked to say more formal prayers. Traditional prayers were recited at important public ceremonial occasions, and these may have been originally composed by past Inca Emperors or high priests. Since sin was considered likely to cause the gods anger and bring bad luck, confession was also a part of worship. The priest who heard confession sometimes tested the truth of it by divination and where lies or half-truths were revealed the would-be confessor was punished by having a stone dropped on his back. Apart from this, the priest usually kept the confessional secrets to himself. When the Incas confessed they did so in private, directly to the Sun, asking for his intercession with the other gods.

Preparation for most festivals and ceremonies, which almost always included worship or cult rituals, required cleansing and fasting by the participants. Most fasting was limited to abstinence from meat, salt, tasty spices in food preparation, and from sexual relations. The fast days before feasts were carefully observed and varied in length from two to six days. Fasting as a penance, or a cure, was also practised under priestly super-vision. Cieza tells us that the most religious of the indians, or the person considered closest to the gods, was asked to fast for a whole year for the good health of everyone. Such a fast might start when the maize was sown and lasted until the crop was harvested. Special fasts were conducted in isolation and retirement by the Emperor before his coronation, or before making important decisions. Such decisions were accompanied by sacrifices to the gods and consultation of the oracles, or by the Calpa divination ceremony.

The *Calpa* ('strength') divination ceremony was performed in preparation for a military campaign. The ceremony consisted of sacrificing a llama (*92*) from which a priest assessed the outcome of the campaign by removing a lung and blowing into a vein, then observing the markings on the surface of the lung. The entrails of the llama were also consulted in assessing a suitable heir for the succession. A few prestigious oracles, such as those of Wari-wilka, Pachacamac, Apu-Rimac (near that river) and Rimac (near

92 Divination: the Sapa Inca consults a priest and, in the Calpa ceremony, the entrails of a llama

Lima) or at the temple of the Island of Titicaca, were consulted by pilgrims from many parts of the empire. In these shrines the images were stained with the blood of sacrifices and priests interpreted the oracles. But any huaca might provide answers to questions concerning illness, lost property, enemies, crimes committed, truthfulness—in short any type of problem. At Conchaca an interesting rock has been discovered in which a carved compartment could have hidden an attendant priest.

Rowe describes a very solemn method of Inca divination, which was also accompanied by sacrifices, for important matters: communication with the spirits was made in this case by means of fire *(92)*. Fires were built in two metal or pottery braziers, placed end to end, and around these dishes of food and drink were set out. With a quid of coca leaves in his mouth the diviner summoned the spirits by chanting and weeping, inviting them to the feast. Accepting voices would then emerge from the fire. It is probable that this feat was performed by ventriloquism, but 'the spirit's statements were ratified by streams of flame issuing from designated openings in the brazier, manipulated, of course, by the assistants with the blowing tubes'.

Omo, local sorcerers, usually secret practitioners of black magic, were feared and quickly condemned by the Incas for any harm they might cause. They were consulted on a variety of smaller problems, and claimed that they spoke directly with spirits in the dark. Typical superstititions also included the sorts of games which are common even today, such as counting to even or odd numbers. However, the pebbles used were usually supposed to have had a magical origin. Movements of animals, especially of spiders, were watched and interpreted and unusual events in the supernatural or natural worlds were seen as omens.

Eclipses and falling stars were seen as bad omens (p. 205). Cobo describes rituals performed at the eclipse of the Moon. The belief was that, when she eclipsed, a puma or a serpent attacked her to break her up—so the people shouted and cried out, whipping their dogs to make them howl and frighten the attacker away. Men prepared themselves as if for battle, blowing their trumpets, banging their drums, and making frightening noises; they shot their arrows and gesticulated with their spears towards the Moon, to make the puma or serpent flee.

Certain noises made by animals, such as the hooting of an owl or the howling of a dog, foretold a death, and certain animals such as snakes, lizards, spiders, toads and moths, when seen about the house, were regarded as bad omens, perhaps because the sorcerers used such creatures. The fox was also considered a bad omen in some parts of the Andean area. Even the fire, if it sparked, might be interpreted as being angry, and had to be appeased with a little chicha.

Dreams could be regarded as important supernatural occurrences, experiences and omens, and these could be analysed.

SACRIFICES

All important occasions were observed by sacrifices, and the public feasts attended by the Inca Emperor to witness them, 'carried out with great celebration'. Types of sacrifices acceptable to the different deities and huacas, varied with the occasion and the priest sometimes selected these by divination.

The most general public sacrifices were of llamas, guinea pigs, or, and this was more rare, of birds or even of humans. The blood of such sacrifices was offered to the idol and smeared over it. *Capaccocha*, human sacrifice', the sacrifice of two infants, was offered every year in the most important temples only. No human blood was shed in less venerated temples, to which gold and silver, also coca leaves, were the most important offerings. Capaccocha was also performed at times of great distress, for example during an Emperor's illness or during times of general famine, war or pestilence. At the coronation of a new Emperor up to 200 children were sacrificed. Cobo tells us that the victims were about ten years old, the boys were taken as taxation, and the girls were picked from those already in the Acllahuasi. The children were sacrificed after being feasted and sometimes they were made drunk. They were either strangled, had their throats cut, or their hearts were cut out.

Sacrificial victims, which had to be without blemishes, were walked around the idol to which they were to be sacrificed. Different coloured llamas were specially selected for some deities: pure white llamas belonged to the Sun, brown ones to Viracocha, and varicoloured ones to the Thunder god. Other sacrifices included coca leaves, maize, cumbi cloth, and special wood-carvings representing human beings, which were cere-moniously burned. Gold and silver ornaments were buried, or hung on the walls of the shrine. After the appropriate number of specified sacrifices had been made out of the huaca's religious stores, that is after the official sacrifices were performed, other personal offerings were accepted and divided between the idol and the priests for the respective up-keep. These private offerings included chicha, specially prepared food, beads, ground or carved shells and feathers. More important, private offerings might include a llama or a guinea pig. Individual offerings also consisted of plucking a few eyebrow hairs or eyelashes, or even blood letting from the lobes of the ears.

Some sacrifices were made to the Sun daily, in the main square of Cuzco. Before sunrise a fire of carved wood was laid, and lit as the Sun appeared; specially prepared food was then thrown in for the Sun to eat. During the day a dark-red llama was sacrificed and burned with coca. In addition, on the first day of every month the Emperor and the élite of inner Cuzco gathered in the Huacapata where 100 llamas were dedicated by the high priest, to Viracocha, in the name of the Sun. These were then divided between 30 attendants, representing the days of the month, each of whom was to bring out, in turn during the month, his share of three or four llamas for sacrifice. At the end of the month all the sacrifices were burned and the bones were ground into powder and stored.

THE CALENDAR AND THE FESTIVALS

The Sun, Moon and Stars were also observed in Inca astronomical studies. The later Inca astronomers had learnt to reconcile their 12 lunar months with 12 solar months, since a cycle of 12 lunar months add up to only 354 days and the solar year is just under 365 days and a quarter.

In the solar calendar the 12 months, including those seasons for the planting and starting of the agricultural year, were calculated from the Sun's appearance on certain stone towers, built especially for this purpose. Twelve of these towers, called *pacaonancaq* (time-markers) were built on high locations to the east and west of Cuzco. (Although some sources suggest there may have been only four towers, marking the equinoxes and solstices.) On the first day of each month the rising of the sun from behind one of the towers was observed from the usnu, in the main square of Cuzco (*91*).

The *Inca* also traditionally counted the lunar months. These were probably used before their disparity with the solar months was recognized, which caused Pachacuti Inca to build towers for solar observation. The lunar months continued to be noted, especially since many rituals were known to be associated with the phases of the moon. In order to coordinate these with the solar months, festivals were celebrated when the moon, for the first time, passed the necessary phase during a solar month.

The Cuzco ceremonial calendar became the state cycle of ceremonies and festivals; the most important events of which were:

Inti Raymi, 'Feast of the Sun', took place at the winter solstice, in June. Great sacrifices were made, on the hills near Cuzco and offered to the Sun. These included burying children alive with silver and golden vessels, powdered sea shells and llamas. This was followed by a banquet celebration, at the Sun's expense, and everyone danced in the public plaza.

Chahua-huarquiz, Chacra Ricuichic or *Chacra Cona*, 'the Ploughing Month', was in July when sacrifices were made to the huaca which presided over the irrigation system of the valley.

Yapaquis, Chacra Ayapui or *Capac Siquis* was the 'Sowing' month — August, when sacrifices were made to all the huacas. After the new maize crop was ceremoniously sown in Mama Huaca's field, sacrifices were also made to the Frost, Air, Water and Sun.

Coya Raymi and *Citua*, 'Feast of the Moon', was celebrated in September at the spring equinox, and Poma tells us that this was the month in which the women most enjoyed themselves. The

Citua festival started at the moment of the appearance of the new moon. The men were responsible for cleansing the city of sickness (p. 94). After the sickness had been dispelled, everyone bathed and maize porridge was smeared on faces and doorway lintels as a symbol of purification. Feasting and dancing followed for several days after which four llamas were sacrificed and their lungs examined for omens. On this occasion all the subject tribes brought their huacas into the Huacapata to acknowledge the Inca Emperor.

K'antaray or *Uma Raymi* was a month corresponding to October, during which the crops were carefully watched. Sacrifices were made to the principal huaca, and if necessary, special ceremonies and sacrifices were held to increase the rainfall.

Ayamarca, corresponding to November, was the month during which the Festival of the Dead was held. The dead were brought out in public for special ceremonies and received offerings and food. The maturity rites began with the candidates spending a night at Huanacauri and making sacrifices.

Capac Raymi, 'Magnificent Festival', included the December solstice when the Huarachico rites were held, after which, the products of the Emperor and Religion were brought into Cuzco from the provinces; followed by much celebration and sacrifices of gold, silver and infants.

Camay quilla: at the new moon in January the Huarachico rites were continued by fasting and penitence, and by the mock battle in the main square, followed by dances and sacrifices. At full moon additional dances and sacrifices were held and the dancers carried the *muru-urco* chain, a great woollen rope of four colours, perhaps representing the four great quarters. Six days later all the previous year's sacrifices were burned and dumped into the river to be carried away to Viracocha.

Hatun-pucuy, 'Great Ripening', took place in a month corresponding to February. At the new moon gold and silver sacrifices were offered first to the Sun, then the Moon and other deities. 'Twenty guinea pigs and 20 loads of firewood were offered to the Sun, for the crops.'

Pacha-puchuy, 'Earth Ripening', took place in a month corresponding to March, the month of the autumn equinox. Fasting was observed and at the new moon attention to the ripening crops was paid and black llamas were sacrificed.

Ayrihua or *Camay Inca Raymi*, in April, was the Festival of the

Inca over which the Sun presided. A ceremony was held in honour of the royal insignia which entailed members of the royal family singing to a sacred llama. This was a perfectly white animal which was dressed as one of them, and which took part in many ceremonies, symbolizing the first llama on earth.

Aymoray quilla or *Hatun Cuzqui*, the 'Great Cultivation', took place in a month corresponding to May. This month's festivals celebrated the maize harvest and its storage. Llamas were sacrificed to the Sun and the huacas and banquets with much drinking of chicha followed. There were many local festivals and rituals enacted. The boys who were due to be ennobled harvested Mama Huaca's field.

In addition, some festivals were held when the need arose, as in the case of *Itu*. The Itu rituals began with fasting, all provincials and dogs were sent out of the city and the images of the deities were brought into the Huacapata. After sacrifices, a procession of young men, specially dressed in red shirts and finery, walked around the square beating small white drums. When they sat down, a noble followed the same path, scattering coca. This performance was repeated eight times and the participants spent the night in the plaza in order to pray to Viracocha and the Sun. A feast followed, lasting for two days.

TIME

Short periods of time, such as the time of day, were assessed by practical means, by the position of the sun, and could be measured by the distance it travelled in the sky. Poma tells us that the Inca week lasted ten days and that three such weeks made a month of 30 days. An extra one or two days were sometimes added.

Zuidema stresses the importance of the ceque system for the calendar. He shows how, associated with each group of three ceques in the region of Cuzco, a tower is found representing a month. The number of huacas in the ceque line might therefore have indicated the days of a week, and these totalled 333. By adding to these the principal temples and towers one gets a total of 350—the inference being that this is very near 365 days and that another method of calculation might solve the descrepancy, making up a year. This subject needs more research.

Longer periods of time were not so carefully observed or calculated. The time span of a ruler's dynasty was thought of as having a fixed number of years—according to Sarmiento's lists, the rulers Manco Capac to Pachacuti Inca reigned for a 100 years each, plus or minus a few years—an adjustment made perhaps to make such claims more credible to the readers of his history. The division of time was based on quinquepartition and decempartition (5 and 10). This system was used theoretically to divide people's lives into approximate age groups of set time, and also to calculate other time spans. In the Inca system of dividing time, five worlds of 1,000 years each had passed. A *Capac-huatan* (1,000 years) was the life span of a Sun, and every Sun was a world divided by two *Pachacutis* (of 500 years each) when great changes were brought about. In Montesino's list of Inca rulers the Inca Pachacuti was the ninth ruler with this name and the fifth world probably began with his reign.

10

Civil war and the Spanish conquest

THE EVENTS OF THE LAST DECADE

During Huayna Capac's reign there were two events that hinted at the confrontation between the Incas and the Spanish that was to come. First, when the Chiriguana attacked the Inca empire from the east they were accompanied by Alejo Garcia, an adventurous Spaniard. The attack was successfully repulsed but this Spaniard, who had made his way from the coast of Brazil, was the first European to visit the Inca empire. Secondly, in 1527, word was brought to Huayna Capac when he was in Quito, that strange bearded men had appeared on the coast from the west. This was Pizarro's preliminary exploratory expedition which touched at Tumbez. In the same year, shortly after this news had been received, there was an epidemic (probably smallpox brought by the Spanish expedition) from which many people died. A victim of the epidemic was the great Huayna Capac, who died without having officially or finally chosen an heir. According to some accounts, on his deathbed the Emperor consulted the oracles but the customary divination ceremonies were not clearly favourable to any of the main candidates. *Ninan* was the eldest son but he was also to die of the pestilence, shortly after his father. *Huascar*, the obvious heir, was in Cuzco where he lost no time in having himself crowned by the high priest before any further political conspiracy could interfere with his inheritance.

Unfortunately, complication followed Huascar's succession. *Atahuallpa*, Huascar's half-brother and his father's favourite illegitimate son, assumed the governorship of Quito province — which he claimed was his father's wish. Atahuallpa seems to have made this claim while at the same time accepting Huascar's authority as Inca Emperor, but Huascar overreacted to this and, rightly or wrongly, feared Atahuallpa as a rival. This situation was aggravated by the news that Atahuallpa was living in a luxury which rivalled that of the Inca himself—a dangerous sign in view of the symbolism attached to the ranking of all such privileges. Furthermore, Huascar was quarrelling with his mother who was doing her utmost to prevent him marrying his sister, his traditional right which would consolidate his position as Inca Emperor. The situation was further complicated by complex political intrigues in Cuzco and in Quito, precipitating the two sides into a civil war. This division was essentially a moiety one between Hanan and Hurin Cuzco. Atahuallpa was supported by Quito and the Hurin Cuzcos, Huascar by the Hanan Cuzcos. Atahuallpa, who had the advantage of his father's most brilliant generals and a well-trained army in Quito, met and defeated Huascar's army after only a few encounters.

Barely had the generals defeated Huascar, captured and imprisoned him in 1532, than news reached Atahuallpa of Pizarro's arrival on the coast. Atahuallpa was waiting in Cajamarca for word from his generals that he could proceed to Cuzco, to take full official control of the government; he had as yet had no time, so soon after the civil war, to consolidate his newly won position as Emperor. His generals, Quisquis and Challcuchima, were busy in Cuzco ruthlessly killing all the leaders and male members of Huascar's faction who might have had more legitimate claims than Atahuallpa to the Incaship. Meanwhile Huascar was still alive in prison.

Atahuallpa does not seem to have particularly feared the Spaniards. He had an overpowering advantage in numbers against a mere 200 of them and so had no reason to feel physically threatened; curiosity, and perhaps an uncertainty as to the true nature of the strangers, led him to allow the Spaniards to reach Cajamarca. Many sources describe how both the Incas and the provincials were initially awestruck by the bearded Spaniards and their horses. The followers of Huascar, who seem to have maintained some resistance to Atahuallpa in the Cuzco region, may have even briefly sought reassurance in the hope that the Spaniards were a contigent of messengers of the civilizing god, Viracocha, who had come to punish Atahuallpa for usurping the legitimate régime.

The Spaniards arrived in Cajamarca, tired and frightened, led by a determined and resourceful leader. Atahuallpa had withdrawn to some hot springs outside the town and left orders that the Spaniards be lodged in the centre of the town. Two conquistadores lost no time in paying Atahuallpa a visit, riding into the army encampment by the hot springs and startling the warriors with their horses. At this meeting it was agreed that Atahuallpa would visit Pizarro on the following day in Cajamarca. Perhaps believing that horses lost their strength at night and confident of his superiority in numbers and the Spaniard's fear, Atahuallpa made a twilight entrance into Cajamarca with 2,000 retainers, as described in Francisco de Jerez's eyewitness account:

> First came a squadron of indians dressed in a red and white check livery, who picked up the straws from the ground and swept the road; then more bands in different liveries, all singing and dancing, and after them a number of men with breastplates, medallions and gold and silver crowns, in the midst of whom came Atahuallpa in a litter lined with multi-coloured parrots' feathers and decorated with gold and silver plates. The prince was borne on the shoulders of many indians [one account says 80 chiefs in blue livery], and behind him came two more litters and two hammocks containing persons of importance, who were followed by many more who wore gold and silver crowns and marched in bands. On entering the square, Atahuallpa made a sign for silence.

Seeing only a few Spaniards, Atahuallpa was suspicious and refused to descend from his litter. The Bishop Vicente de Valverde then came forward to make a speech demanding recognition of the Christian faith and the Emperor Charles v, which was crudely translated by an interpreter. Atahuallpa naturally showed no humility and did not submit to such ridiculous demands; on the contrary, he was annoyed and indignant. What followed, the slaughter of the retainers and his capture by the Spaniards, happened quickly—a coup brilliantly planned by Pizarro before the army outside the town could intervene. With the Emperor's safety uncertain and without the leadership of its most effective generals, the army was transfixed and uncertain what to do.

The Spaniards were able to achieve what they did in this encounter, and those that followed, by the element of surprise, the panic inspired by their horses, cannons and the psychological effect of their assumed divinity. An additional and important factor was that Pizarro obtained the help of the legitimate faction of the Incas and of tribes like the Cañari, who opposed Inca domination. By the time the Andean realized the true intentions of the Spaniards it was too late.

The events that followed the capture of Atahuallpa led up to the full realization and shock of the conquest for the Andean people. Atahuallpa secretly ordered the death of Huascar, who was also negotiating for his freedom with the Spaniards. The latter then availed themselves of this fact as an excuse to get rid of Atahuallpa, whose continuing presence and authority might cause a general uprising. His trial, on a number of unrealistic charges, was quickly followed by execution by strangulation. For the Andeans this meant an end to their world: the Inca Emperor, in his role of Son of the Sun, was the point of reference from which the world was organized and through which men's communication with the gods was assured. The people experienced this event as something cataclysmic, as expressed in a sixteenth-century elegy: 'The earth refused to devour the Inca's body—rocks trembled—tears made torrents, the Sun was obscured—the Moon ill.' (93)

The records describe many Inca stories of bad omens foreshadowing the arrival of the Spaniards and the subsequent fall of the empire. During the reign of Huayna Capac the empire was unduly troubled by earthquakes and tidal waves; Huayna Capac himself made prophecies. In Huascar's brief reign, during the feast of the Sun, a condor was pursued by falcons and fell into the middle of the great plaza of Cuzco; the bird was found to be suffering from disease and no amount of care could cure it. The

93 The execution of Atahuallpa in Cajamarca was depicted by Poma as decapitation; in fact he was garotted and it was Topa Amaru (page 207) who was decapitated later

moon also foretold the disaster when she was seen on a clear night surrounded by a triple halo; the first band of the colour of blood, the second black and the third like smoke. A diviner interpreted the omen: blood announced war between the descendants of Huayna Capac, black signified ruin of the Religion and the Inca empire which would go out in smoke. Such prophecies and interpretations of omens may have been made retrospectively, and as Nathan Watchel suggests, perhaps in an effort to better interpret the event of the conquest which had so shattered their world.

EVENTS AFTER THE FALL OF THE INCA EMPIRE

After the execution of Atahuallpa, Pizarro selected a puppet Inca, young *Topa Huallpa*, a brother of Huascar, but he was soon disposed of, poisoned by Challcuchima who wished to see a brother of Atahuallpa's crowned. Pizarro then chose *Manco Inca*, another of Huayna Capac's sons. Manco Inca respected an alliance with the Spanish until 1536, when, after a series of public humiliations, he chose to strike back. While Pizarro was at the new Spanish capital of Lima, and Diego de Almagro, the other Spanish leader was in Chile, Manco Inca, with the pretext of fetching a golden statue to Cuzco, left to organize an uprising. He returned to Cuzco with 50,000 men and nearly succeeded in taking it. A few Spaniards managed to hold out but the indians held control of most of the town and the fortress of Sacahuaman for almost a year. Eventually the siege failed and Manco Inca had to withdraw to Ollantaytambo, from which in turn he was later dislodged. Finally, he withdrew with some supporters into the region of Vilcabamba, where he maintained the cult of the *Inca* and restored their religion in a temple at Vitcos. From this hinterland the rebels continually harassed the Spaniards.

A new puppet Inca, *Paullu Topa Inca*, was invested by Almagro while Manco Inca maintained his neo-Inca state. By 1557, under Manco Inca's son *Sayri Topa*, the Inca state covered an immense territory from Huánuco to Cuzco including the montaña and the fringe hot lands. The Antisuyus living in this area still paid tribute to the Inca.

The shock of the conquest continued throughout the colonial period, which saw the founding of Spanish towns and the take-over of all the lands of the Emperor and the Religion by the Spanish settlers; in addition, increased demands in tribute and mit'a work were made of the indian population. Spain governed the country by continuing to use the existing institutions when it suited them to do so and by leaving others to decay. The introduction of money and the elimination of reciprocity was particularly confusing and had disastrous effects on the Andeans. With the destruction of Inca ritual, of their gods and religious ideas, the discipline of the cultivation ritual disappeared and the indians, who formed the basis of the Spanish colonial economy, were forced to conform by their local curacas, who were in turn pressured into exploiting the indians by the new local land-owners.

While the Spanish settlers introduced a number of new products, such as wheat, barley, varieties of fruits and of vege-tables, and a range of domestic animals including chickens, pigs, sheep, goats, cattle and horses, few of these were easily accepted into the indigenous culture. In fact, Nathan Watchel stresses the fact that most Andeans sought to express their repudiation of their new rulers through a rejection of their culture—a resistance that has continued in varying degrees in many parts of the former Inca empire until this day.

In 1560 *Sayri Topa*, who was enticed to return to Cuzco and resume his role under the Spanish authorities, died of poisoning and his half-brother *Titu Cusi* succeeded him in Vilcabamba. During his reign the rebel Inca state threatened Spanish security and was probably behind the *Taqui Ongo*, a politico-religious resurgence movement. In 1565, a planned revolt was discovered and squashed, and as a consequence of this Spanish repression became more violent.

The existence of the neo-Inca state continued to threaten Spanish security, although perhaps only theoretically, so that the new Viceroy Francisco de Toledo determined in 1572 to put an end to this threat. He organized a decisive expedition into the forested mountains of the Vilcabamba. Young *Topa Amaru*, the legitimate son of Manco Inca, had taken over the Incaship only a year previously. He was caught unprepared and fled towards the tropical forest with his family, where he was finally run to earth and captured. Topa Amaru's captors took this Inca and his family back to Cuzco, leading them on foot into the town. The young Inca was decapitated in public before the royal family, who were increasingly persecuted in the years to follow. At his public execution Topa Amaru surprised everyone present by denouncing his traditional gods and receiving the baptism. To the Andeans this event was a symbolic repetition of the disastrous death of Atahuallpa, the event that marked the real destruction of the Inca world and was followed by domination of a totally foreign culture, with its incomprehensible demands and values.

Bibliography

With English translations of Spanish Sources

Bandelier, A. F. A. 1910. *The Islands of Titicaca and Koati.* The Hispanic Society of America, New York

Betanzos, Juan de 1880. *Suma y narración de los Incas* ... (1551). Biblioteca Hispano-Ultramarina, vol. 5, Madrid

Bingham, Hiram 1930, *Machu Picchu, Citadel of the Incas.* Memoires of the National Geographic Society. Yale Univ. Press, New Haven

*Bushnell, G. H. S. 1963 (2nd edition). *Peru.* Ancient peoples and places series Thames & Hudson, London

Chávez Ballón, M. 1970. *Ciudades Incas: Cuzco Capital del Imperio.* Wayka, no. 3, Departamento de Antropologia, Univ. Nac. del Cuzco, Peru.

Cieza de Léon, Pedro de (Crónica del Perù... (1551). 1864. *The Travels of Peter de Cieza.* Ed. by Clements Markham. Hakluyt Society, vol. XXXIII, London 1883. The second part of the *Chronicle of Peru*, 1532–50. Ed. by Clements Markham. Hakluyt Society, vol. LXVIII. London

1913. *The War of Quito and Inca Documents.* Ed. by Clements Markham. Hakluyt Society, 2nd ser., no. XXXI, London

*1959. *The Incas of Pedro Cieza de León.* Ed. by Victor W. von Hagen. Transl. by Harriet de Onis. Civilization of the American Indian Series. Univ. of Oklahoma, Norman.

Cobo, Bernabé 1956, *Historia del nuevo mundo* (1653). Ed. P. Francisco Mateos. Biblioteca de autores españoles, vols. LXXXXI, LXXXXII, Madrid. Ed. Lius A. Pardo, Publicaciones Pardo-Galimberti, Vols. III and IV,(1956), Cuzco, Peru

D'Harcourt, Raoul 1962. *Textiles of ancient Peru and their techniques.* Univ. Washington Press

Fejos, Paul 1944. *Archaeological Explorations in the Cordillera Vilcabamba.* Viking Fund Publi. in Anthropology, no. 3. New York. (1963, Johnson Reprint)

Garci Diez De San Miguel 1964. *Visita que se hizo de los Indios de la Provincia de Chucuito* (1567–8). Documentos Regionales para la Etnologia y Etnohistoria Andina, vol. I. Casa de la Cultura del Perú, Lima

Garcilaso De La Vega, El Inca (Commentarios Reales de los Incas 1609 & 1617)

1869, 1871. First Part of the *Royal Commentaries of the Incas.* Ed. by Clements Markham. Hakluyt Society vols. XXXXI, XXXXV. London

*1966. *Royal Commentaries of the Incas.* Trans. by Harold V. Livermore. Texas Pan American Series, Austin & London.

Handbook of South American Indians, vol. 2. 1946. Julian H. Steward editor. Smithsonian Institution, Bureau of American Athnology Bulletin 143, Washington DC.

Harth-Terré, Emilio 1964. *El Pueblo de Huánuco Viejo.* Arquitecto Peruano no. 320/21. Lima

*Jones, J. 1969. *Art of Empire: the Inca of Peru.* Museum of Primitive Art. New York

Izikowitz, K. G. 1935. *Musical Instruments of the South American Indians,* a comparative ethnographical study. Goteborg. (Reprint available)

Markham, Sir Clements 1872. Reports on the Discovery of Peru (Francisco de Xerex, Miguel de Estete, Hernando Pizarro, Pedro Sancho). Haklyut Society. vol. XXXXVII. London

Macneish, R. S. 1969. First Annual Report, 1970 Second Annual Report, Ayacucho Archaeological-Botanical Project, both Publ. Peabody Foundation for Archaeology, Andover, Mass.

1970. *Early Man in the Andes.* Scientific American

Molina (El Cuzqueno), Cristobal de, 1943. *Falulas y ritos de los Incas* (1573). Ed. Los pequeños grandes libros de historia americana, ser. I, vol. IV. Lima.

1873. *The Fables and Rites of the Incas.* Ed. by Clements Markham. In: Hakluyt Society vol. XXXXVIII. London.

Montell, G. 1929. *Dress and Ornaments in Ancient Peru.* Elanders Boktryckeri Aktiebolag. Goteborg

Murra, John V. 1960. Rite and Crop in the Inca state. In: *Culture in History: Essays in Honour of Paul Radin* (Stanley Diamond, editor) pp. 393–407. Columbia Univ. Press. New York

1962. *Cloth and its functions in the Inca state.* American Anthropologist, vol. 64, no. 4 pp. 710–728

1965. Herds and Herders in the Inca state. In: *Man, Culture, and Animals.* Publ. no. 78. American Assoc. for the advancement of Science, Washington DC.

1961. Guaman Poma de Ayala. In: *Natural History,* Part I-August, Part 2-September

Murúa (Morúa), Martín de 1964. *Historia General del Perú* (1613). Colección Joyas Bibliograficas, Biblioteca Americana Vetus, vols. I & II. Madrid

Ocampo, Baltasar de (1610. Descripción de la provincia de San Francisco de la Vitoria de Vilcapampa)

1907. *Account of the Province of Vilcapampa and a Narrative of the Execution of the Inca Tupac Amaru.* Ed. by Cl. Markham. Hakluyt Society, 2nd ser., XXII pp. 203–47

Pachacuti Yamqui Salcamaygua, Juan de Santacruz 1950. (1879 edition) *Relación de antiguedades deste reyno del Pirú* (1613). Tres relaciones de antiguedades peruanas. pp. 207–281. Ascunsion del Paraguay

1873. *An account of the antiquitius of Peru.* Ed. Cl. Markham. Hakluyt Society vol. XXXVIII pp. 67–120. London

Pizarro, Pedro 1944. *Relación del descubrimiento y conquista de los reinos del Perú* (1571). Editorial Futuro, 2nd edition, Buenos Aires.

Poma de Ayala, F. Guamán 1936. *Nueva corónica y buen gobierno* (1615). Institut d'Ethnologie, Paris

Rowe, John Howland 1944. An introduction to the archaeology of Cuzco. Papers of the Peabody Museum of American Archaeology and Ethnology, Harvard Univ., vol. XXVII, no. 2. Cambridge

1946. Inca culture at the time of the Spanish Conquest. *Handbook of South American Indians*, vol. 2. pp 183–330 (see above)

1967. *What kind of settlement was Inca Cuzco?* Nawpa Pacha 7, Institute of Andean Studies, Berkeley, California

Rowe & Menzel 1967. *Peruvian Archaeology: Selected Readings.* Peek Publications. California

Sancho, Pedro 1917, *An account of the Conquest of Peru.* Transl. by P. A. Means. The Cortez Society. New York.(Kraus Reprint 1968)

Sarmiento de Gamboa, Pedro de (Historia indica 1572)

1907. *History of the Incas.* Ed. by Cl. Markham, Hakluyt Society, 2nd ser., vol. XXII, Cambridge

Thompson, D. E. 1968. Incaic installations at Huánuco and Pumpu. Proc. of the XXXIIth Int. Congress of Americanists, Argentina, vol. I, p. 67. Buenos Aires

1968. *An Archaeological Evaluation of Ethnohistorical Evidence of Inca Culture.* Ed. Meggers, Anthropological Archaeology, Anthropological Society, Washington

Tschopik, Harry Jr. 1946. The Aymara. In: *Handbook of South American Indians*, vol. 2. pp. 501–573. (See above)

*Watchel, Nathan 1971. *La Vision des Vaincus*—Les indiens du Perou devant la conquête espanole. Bibliotheque de l'histoire nouvelle. Gallimard

*Zárate, Augustín de 1968. *Discovery and conquest of Peru* (1555). Transl. by J. M. Cohen. Penguin

Zuidema, R. T. 1962. The relationship between mountains and coast in ancient Peru. In: *Mededelingen van het Rijksmuseum voor Volkenkunde*, Leiden, no. 15. Leiden

1964. *The Ceque System of Cuzco.* Suppl. to vol. I, Int. Archives of Ethnography, Transl. by E. M. Hooykaas, Leiden

1966. *El Calendario Inca.* Proc. XXXVI Int. Congress of Americanists, vol. 2. pp. 25–30. Sevilla

1968. *A visit to God*

*General Selection for further reading:

Bingham; H: *Lost City of the Incas* (NY 1948; London 1951)

Guerra, F: *The Pre-Columbian Mind* (Seminar Press London & NY)

Hagen, V. von: *Highway of the Sun* (NY 1957)

Hardoy, J: *Urban Planning in pre-Columbian America* (Studio Vista, London 1968)

Hemming, J: *The Conquest of the Incas* (MacMillan 1970)

Innes, H: *The Conquistadores* (Thames & Hudson 1970)

Kosok; P: *Life' Land and Water in Ancient Peru* (Long Isl. Univ. Press NY. 1965)

Lanning, E: *Peru before the Incas* (Prentice-Hall NJ 1967)

Moore, S. Falk: *Power and Property in Inca Peru* (Columbia Univ. Press NY 1958)

Osborne, H: *South American Indian Mythology* (Hamlyn 1968)

Swanson, Earl H., Bray, W., Farrington, I. *The New World* (Elsevier, Oxford, 1976)

Willey, G. S. *Introduction to American Archaeology*, vol. 2. South America. (Prentice-Hall NJ 1972)

INCA DYNASTY

    (Spanish spelling)

1.   Manco Capac
2.   Sinchi Roca
3.   Lloque Yupanqui
4.   Mayta Capac
5.   Capac Yupanqui
6.   Inca Roca
7.   Yahuar Huacac
8.   Viracocha Inca
–.   Inca Urcon
9.   Pachacuti Inca Yupanqui 1438–1471
10.   Topa Inca Yupanqui 1471–1493
11.   Huayna Capac 1493–1525
12.   Huascar 1525–1532
      Atahuallpa 1532–1533
      Topa Huallpa 1532–
13.   Manco Inca Yupanqui 1533–1545
      Paullu Topa Inca
      Topa Amaru 1545–1572
      Sayri Topa 1545–1558
14.   Titu Cusi Yupanqui 1558–1571
      (after Rowe, 1961)

INDEX